Expertise, Policy-making and Democracy

This book offers a concise and accessible introduction to debates about expertise, policy-making and democracy. It uniquely combines an overview of recent research on the policy role of experts with discussions in political philosophy and the philosophy of expertise. Starting with the fact that well-functioning democracies require experts and expert knowledge, the book examines two types of objections against granting experts a larger role in policy-making: concerns that focus on the nature and limits of expert knowledge, and those that concentrate on tensions between expertization and democracy. With this, the book discusses how expert arrangements can be organized to ensure the epistemic qualities of policies and democratic credentials, at the same time.

The book will be of interest to scholars and students of political theory and democracy, public policy and administration, and to anyone interested in the role of expertise in society.

Johan Christensen is Assistant Professor at the Institute of Public Administration at Leiden University, The Netherlands.

Cathrine Holst is Professor at the Department of Sociology and Human Geography at the University of Oslo, Norway.

Anders Molander is Professor at the Centre for the Study of Professions at Oslo Metropolitan University, Norway.

Routledge Studies in Governance and Public Policy

Expertise, Policy-making and Democracy

Johan Christensen
Cathrine Holst
Anders Molander

Routledge
Taylor & Francis Group

LONDON AND NEW YORK

First published 2023
by Routledge
4 Park Square, Milton Park, Abingdon, Oxon OX14 4RN

and by Routledge
605 Third Avenue, New York, NY 10158

Routledge is an imprint of the Taylor & Francis Group, an informa business

© 2023 Johan Christensen, Cathrine Holst and Anders Molander

The right of Johan Christensen, Cathrine Holst and Anders Molander to be
identified as authors of this work has been asserted in accordance with
sections 77 and 78 of the Copyright, Designs and Patents Act 1988.

Trademark notice: Product or corporate names may be trademarks or registered trademarks,
and are used only for identification and explanation without intent to infringe.

British Library Cataloguing-in-Publication Data
A catalogue record for this book is available from the British Library

ISBN: 978-0-367-61776-9 (hbk)
ISBN: 978-0-367-61787-5 (pbk)
ISBN: 978-1-003-10655-5 (ebk)

DOI: 10.4324/9781003106555

Typeset in Times New Roman
by Newgen Publishing UK

Contents

Preface

This book is the culmination of our combined efforts over the past years to better understand the relationship between expertise, policy-making and democracy. All chapters offer a substantial amount of new material, but we also rely on arguments developed elsewhere. The introduction draws on the introduction to a book in Norwegian by Johan Christensen and Cathrine Holst (*Ekspertenes inntog*, 2020). The idea of the fact of expertise (Chapter 1), some points in our discussion of expertise in democratic theory (Chapter 3), the lists of epistemic and democratic worries about expertise (in Chapters 4 and 5), and the three sets of measures to improve on experts' performance (Chapter 6) have been introduced in previous publications (see Holst and Molander 2017, 2018, 2020, 2021).

We are grateful for comments on different parts of the manuscript from colleagues under the research projects: Expertization of public inquiry commissions (EUREX, Research Council of Norway); What is a good policy? Political morality, feasibility and democracy (GOODPOL, Centre for Advanced Studies, Oslo); Policy, expertise and trust (PEriTiA, Horizon 2020) and Experts in Nordic policy-making – increasingly powerful? (NEXPO, UiO:Nordic). Project funding from UiO:Nordic, Centre for Advanced Studies in Oslo and the European Union's research and innovation programme under grant agreement No. 870883 was essential for the writing of this book. Open access publication was supported by grants from UiO:Nordic and Centre for Advanced Studies.

Introduction

During the coronavirus crisis, the presence of experts in policy-making was on vivid display. Experts stood side by side with ministers during weekly – sometimes daily – government press briefings, giving us facts and estimates, but also telling us what to do and not to do ("stop hugging", "stay home from school", "do not leave your country"). Before the pandemic, the British politician Michael Gove famously claimed that people had "had enough of experts".[1] During the crisis, most politicians rather emphasized that "we need to listen to the experts". Across the world, a plethora of government agencies, research institutes and expert groups provided governments with analyses and recommendations about how to contain the spread of the virus and manage the social and economic consequences of the pandemic.

The corona situation *was* extraordinary. Experts are often less visibly present in political life and in the public sphere in normal times, and it is well known how experts are consulted more, and more easily rise to power, in times of crisis. When things are confusing and uncertain, it may be tempting to leave priorities and decisions to the presumably most knowledgeable.

Still, also during ordinary times, public policies and decisions often rely heavily on experts and expert knowledge. In many respects, the coronavirus crisis was *not* that exceptional. We can also see it as a powerful reminder and illustration of how policies are normally made, or at least how contemporary policy-making increasingly takes place.

A plethora of experts are asked for policy advice all the time, and not only on corona and other health issues. Political processes leading up to decisions about tax and pension reforms, new environmental policies, educational policies, family policies, or policies in almost any other domain are often crowded with people with expert knowledge. They may be lawyers, economists or other social scientists, medical specialists, natural scientists and engineers, depending on the policy area and issue.

DOI: 10.4324/9781003106555-1

They may be university professors or researchers at institutes or bureaus who are involved in policy-relevant research, in science advice or in expert committees. They may be civil servants in ministries or agencies, or specialists working for interest groups or civil society organizations, in think tanks or consultancy firms. Most often they have a higher academic degree, and many even have a PhD.

To be sure, during the coronavirus crisis, we also saw how politicians do not always follow experts' advice. In some countries, politicians dismissed expert warnings as alarmist and took a laxer approach than advised by experts. This was not only true for populist leaders such as former US President Trump and Brazil's President Bolsonaro. Many governments were at times unwilling to endorse expert calls for radical measures such as lockdowns or school closures, including in countries such as Belgium and the Netherlands that were hard hit by corona. In other countries, such as Norway and Denmark, politicians opted for stricter lockdown measures than recommended by epidemiologists and expert authorities.

That political leaders do not always listen to experts is not surprising. Research reports, science-based analyses and expert advice may be put aside because politicians disagree with or dislike the approach or conclusions, find the advice irrelevant or unimportant, do not understand or are unaware of what the experts are saying, or find the timing to be wrong or the societal or political costs to be too high. Experts may recommend this or that measure, a reform, a new piece of legislation – but in the end, politicians may want or need something different.

In other cases, the policies adopted are more in line with expert analyses and advice. It is often said with Francis Bacon that "knowledge itself is power". Experts may possess knowledge that enables them to set a new agenda, shape how a societal problem is conceived, and define specific solutions. Politicians may lack both clear ideas about what the problem is and strong views about how to address it, and in such cases, they may easily go along with what experts propose. In economic policy, there are several examples of how economists and financial expert authorities have successfully pushed for policy change at odds with the initial priorities of both politicians and interest groups. But this dynamic is also visible in other areas, and most recently during the coronavirus pandemic, when public health experts were given immense agenda setting power and influence over governance and social planning.

Furthermore, experts are not only more or less powerful political advisors; they may also be delegated decision-making power. Many countries have delegated decisions over interest rates to independent central banks, and a range of other more detailed policy decisions in numerous policy areas have been left to semi-independent agencies and other expert bodies. Similar powers have been given to international and transnational expert institutions that are even further removed from citizens, such as the European Central Bank and the more than 40 agencies of the European Union (EU). In addition to executive organizations comes the power of the legislative expertise of national and international courts. Parliaments legislate, but laws must be interpreted. And the more indeterminacy concerning the application to specific cases, the more power to jurists and judges.

Some argue that even more decisions should be left to experts. During the pandemic, some observers called for the suspension of politics so that medical experts could make the right decisions about public health measures. Similarly, some environmentalists think that the decisions needed to "save the planet" should be left to panels of climate scientists rather than to short-sighted politicians, while some economists argue that decisions about tax policies should be delegated to councils of economic experts to ensure sound policies and a stable economic environment for businesses and individuals.

For others, extensive delegation to experts raises the question of whether experts have too much political power. During the coronavirus crisis, we saw protesters rally against experts and the measures they imposed, urging people to listen less to experts and rather trust their own judgment.

Yet, the simplest answers to questions regarding expert power are not very instructive – and this was seldom more obvious than during the pandemic. To put it bluntly: in a pandemic, when a disease is spreading and a growing number of people get sick and die, most people understand that it may be a good idea to lend an ear to those who study diseases. However, this does not imply that epidemiologists and virologists, or medical experts generally, know more about all things than most other people. Even when it comes to epidemic diseases and measures to contain them, there is a lot a medical expert has little knowledge about, such as the consequences for the economy, children's welfare, mental health or socially disadvantaged groups, or how to weigh economic and social costs and restrictions on civil liberties against disease and mortality rates. Yet, epidemiologists have more substantive knowledge than most on how a virus spreads, and on how to stop or contain its diffusion.

Those who tried to read reports on the coronavirus from expert groups or authorities, and who consulted the scientific studies and research articles on which these reports were based, will probably have seen that the expert knowledge in question may be quite esoteric, technical and sometimes counterintuitive. It can be hard to immediately understand what these studies say, and a Google search or casual reading may not be of much help. Of course, we may have come across a virologist who is a brilliant communicator, and felt that we understood more of how a virus spreads listening to her, but irrespective of experts' communication skills, and how clever we are, and whether we have higher education or not, most of us will not be able to directly assess the validity of a virologist's explanations and judgments since we are not ourselves experts in the field.

Still, we are often told that we should scrutinize what experts say critically and independently, and we may want to do this, and we should definitely do it when we can. However, it is not always easy. To judge arguments based on expert knowledge, you often have to be an expert yourself. Obviously, we can look for indications that make it more likely that a putative expert is in fact a "real" expert. For instance, if someone has a position at a well-reputed research institute or has written articles in peer–reviewed journals, this increases the person's trustworthiness as an expert. At the same time, if you are not yourself an expert on the issue in question or familiar with the relevant research, you will often have a hard time distinguishing good from not-so-good scientific journals and reputed from not-so-well-reputed research institutes. On this inadequate basis, we still need to decide whether the expert in question is a reliable expert or not, and whether he or she is worth listening to as someone especially knowledgeable.

It gets even trickier when a different expert that also seems to have the right merits gives advice that points in a completely different direction. Expert disagreements of this kind were common during the pandemic: where one professor recommended heavier lockdown policies, another called for a more liberal approach. That still other professors wrote petitions or made campaigns advising us to listen to some experts and not to others, did not make our situation easier.

Thus, to simply subscribe to giving "more power to experts" does not bring us very far, and a general advice of just "doing what the experts tell you" is rather unwise. Also, the difficulty lies not only in identifying and listening to the "real" experts (instead of amateurs or quasi-experts). Even experts with the right kind of merits and skills can be biased and mistaken. For instance, they may let their recommendations be determined by the preferences of politicians. The experts who advised the British prime minister Boris Johnson to postpone the lockdown in spring 2020 were criticized for being too concerned with what the politicians wanted and with polls showing that people did not want hard measures instead of relying on their best expert knowledge.

Experts may also be so locked into their disciplinary culture that they fail to see the limitations of their own intellectual perspective or the value of competing approaches. Consider, for instance, the response of epidemiologists to mass demonstrations during the pandemic: such gatherings were potential super-spreader events and should therefore have been prohibited. By contrast, legal experts emphasized demonstrators' fundamental rights to freedom of expression and association, while some political scientists saw the demonstrations as an important form of democratic participation and voice.

We also see how expert advice can vary between countries, even between countries with similar political culture and social institutions. For instance, in the Nordic countries, the Swedish expert authorities recommended markedly softer measures than their counterparts in Denmark, Finland and Norway during the first phase of the pandemic. And while many expert authorities promoted mask-wearing, the Dutch public health agency was for a long time skeptical about the effectiveness of face masks, partly based on the argument that people wearing masks would be less careful about social distancing. To be sure, public health experts probably agreed on a lot regarding the coronavirus and corona measures, irrespective of nationality. Still, expert recommendations varied across nations during all phases of the pandemic, with significant effects on the spread of disease and on people's lives and livelihoods. If the advice is simply "do as the experts tell you", which national experts are we wise to put our trust in?

In the end, even if experts' knowledge about the coronavirus and its effects developed with impressive speed, their models, predictions and recommendations were shaky because we dealt with a pandemic no one had experienced before. Even in the fourth or fifth wave of the pandemic in Europe, the forecasts of some public health agencies about the pressure on intensive care hospital beds were way off the mark.

When all is said and done, we are stuck with listening to these experts, even when they have limited knowledge and disagree, and we inevitably depend on their specialist competence when we make decisions and develop policies, whether we like it or not. And "we" in this case are all of us as citizens. Under a democratic rule where free and equal citizens themselves are supposed to authorize collective decisions, there are limitations on how many big decisions can be delegated to experts without undermining the project of self-government. Even in times of crisis, there are limits to such delegation. In fact, crises raise a range of genuinely *political* questions, meaning questions that involve the use of coercive power and where there are conflicting concerns. In a democracy, we would typically want our elected representatives to assess and weigh these concerns, and as citizens we want to have a voice in political deliberations ourselves as well.

We have reason to value expertise, but also to fear expert power. So, where are we to draw the line? How much expert power is in our interest? This is a problem that democracies have to face, as Carr-Saunders and Wilson drastically put it already in 1933 in their book *Professions*: "Unless the modern world works out a satisfactory relationship between expert knowledge and popular control the days of democracy are numbered" (Carr-Saunders and Wilson 1933, 486).

The content of the book

The role of experts in policy-making in a democratic society is precisely the topic of this book. More specifically, we ask: *which problems does the involvement of experts in policy-making raise for democracy and good governance, and how can they be addressed?*

In examining these questions, the book marries high theory with a discussion of the on-the-ground reality of expert involvement in policy and democracy. The presence of experts in governance and decision-making raises fundamental questions of political philosophy and democratic theory. But the central role of expert knowledge in present-day policy-making is also a salient real-world phenomenon, under intense investigation in empirical research, and a topic for public controversy and debate. It is demanding to bring these different research frontiers and levels of abstraction into conversation. Yet, we believe it is worthwhile, and even essential, at a time when normative political theory and empirical scholarship seem to be drifting further apart.

Our contention is, on the one hand, that philosophical interrogations can give structure, standards and accuracy to empirical investigations and ongoing debates about expertise, policy and democracy. There is a lot of talk in contemporary political discourse and study about the problem of governance by "elites" and "experts" and driven by "evidence". Something vital seems to be at stake, but what precisely is there to worry about? Wherein lies the deeper urgency? For instance, public policy scholars have become increasingly concerned with the democratic problems raised by evidence-based policy-making. Yet, they have made limited headway in analyzing these problems, since they seldom root their normative assessments and prescriptions in philosophical discussions on expertise and democracy. Our book seeks to fill this gap.

On the other hand, empirical knowledge about how expertise is actually incorporated into policy-making can make philosophical debates about expertise and democracy more politically relevant. Philosophical inquiries that do not take basic features of our political reality into account will easily end up being beside the point. We therefore seek to contribute to the philosophical literature by anchoring normative debates in actual institutional arrangements and practices: what are the concrete problems posed by current patterns of expert involvement in policy-making, and what can be done to mitigate them?

Chapter 1 sets out the fundamental premise of the book, namely that well-functioning modern democracies can simply not do without expert knowledge and expert arrangements. We refer to this as "the fact of expertise". Not only do decision-makers nowadays draw extensively on expert advice; relying on expert knowledge also seems to be a condition for *good* political decision-making in today's complex and specialized societies. The chapter outlines our idea of expertise as a "fact" and clarifies the terms "expert" and "expertise".

Chapter 2 describes what this strong and growing expert reliance looks like in practice. Drawing on a broad range of empirical literature on expertise and policy-making, the chapter provides an overview of the manifold channels, mechanisms and arrangements through which expert knowledge is incorporated into political decision-making in contemporary democracies. The chapter also discusses how patterns of expert involvement in policy-making vary across national governments and key international organizations.

Chapter 3 elaborates central contributions in political philosophy on the role of knowledge and the knowledgeable in political rule, but zooms in on recent discussions in normative political theory about "epistemic democracy": the idea that democracy is not only about fair procedures of decision-making, but also about of the quality of decisions. Some worry that this outcome-oriented approach to the justification of government might pave the way for "epistocracy", a rule of the knowers. However, rather than contrasting democracy and epistocracy as political regimes along the lines of recent exchange in political philosophy, we are concerned with expert arrangements *in* contemporary democratic societies. We argue that the fact of expertise is something any adequate theory of democracy must take seriously.

Democracies' dependence on expert arrangements creates a deep and genuine problem for democratic legitimacy, and in Chapters 4 and 5, we survey different types of objections to a large role for experts in policy-making. We group them into epistemic and democratic concerns. The first type of objections focuses on the nature and limits of expert knowledge, and how this may endanger policy and decision quality. The second type of objections sees expertization as a threat against democracy itself, understood as the self-rule of a community of equal citizens.

We outline the different concerns conceptually, but also illustrate the objections and worries with examples from the real world of experts in politics. Our illustrations draw on a wide range of empirical studies, including our own original research.

Finally, Chapter 6 discusses measures against expert misrule and to mitigate democratic worries, relying on a rich set of examples. How can expert arrangements, but also the broader polity, be organized so as to ensure epistemic quality of policies and decisions while at the same time adhering to democratic standards? We present three types of measures that are essential to ensure experts' epistemic performance – measures that target experts' behavior, their judgments, and the organization of expert bodies and advice. In response to the democratic worries, we discuss proposals for "democratizing expertise", but also requirements to a political system that is organized so as to safeguard both democratic and epistemic credentials.

Note

1 The full quote is: "I think people of this country have had enough of experts from organisations with acronyms saying that they know what is best and getting it consistently wrong" (June 3, 2016).

1 The fact of expertise

Imagine that you are the prime minister of a government that has just come to power. Your government is immediately faced with a range of issues that need to be addressed. There are urgent issues, such as an ongoing pandemic, a war in a not-so-far-away country, or rapidly rising prices on gas and electricity. There are also long-standing problems that require your attention, such as the quality of the education system, the emissions of climate gases or the thorny question of immigration. How do you go about dealing with these issues? You quickly realize that the overarching priorities and policy positions established in your election manifesto will only get you so far. For each of the issues faced by your government, more information is needed on the causes of the problem and on possible courses of action and the likely effects of the different interventions. What is causing the sudden surge in virus infections and hospitalizations? How will it affect the energy market if you impose a maximum price on gas and electricity? What interventions will be most effective to reach the targets for emission reductions: tax breaks for renewable energies or curbing emissions from agriculture?

The ministers in your cabinet are all seasoned politicians, with a good grasp of a broad range of policy issues acquired through a long political career. Most of them also have higher education; there are even a few who have a PhD and briefly worked as professors. Yet, the combined knowledge of your cabinet is not close to sufficient to answer any of these questions. On each of the issues, you depend fundamentally on the input of experts with specialized knowledge about the workings of the human body and mind, the economic system or the global environment.

This reliance on expert knowledge at the core of contemporary governance and decision-making may be deeply frustrating for politicians (when they want something that goes against the evidence) or experienced as a relief (when appeal to expert authority protects politicians from decision pressures). Yet, it seems unavoidable, and in what follows, we

DOI: 10.4324/9781003106555-2

will argue that it is a "fact" of contemporary political life similar to "the fact of reasonable pluralism" which is at the center of John Rawls's political liberalism.

General facts of modern societies

In *Political Liberalism*, John Rawls identifies a set of "general facts" that he considers to be characteristic of modern societies. By "facts", Rawls means deep-seated and enduring features of such societies that any applicable political philosophy must come to terms with. The most basic of Rawls's "general facts" is the fact of "reasonable pluralism": "A modern society is characterized not only by a pluralism of comprehensive religious, philosophical, and moral doctrines, but by a pluralism of incompatible yet reasonable comprehensive doctrines" (Rawls 1993, xviii). Doctrines are "comprehensive", according to Rawls, when they include "conceptions of what is of value in human life, and ideals of personal character, as well as ideals of friendship and of familial and associational relationships" (13). They are "incompatible" in that they are based on ideals that may conflict. For instance, whereas one comprehensive doctrine can value community above individual self-realization, or regard religion as an indispensable part of a valuable way of life, another values individual freedom over community and religion. Yet, the doctrines in question are also "reasonable" when they acknowledge that there is a pluralism of reasonable comprehensive doctrines in modern societies, and that this must be taken into account when making claims on others (1993, 58 ff.).[1] "Reasonable pluralism" is a permanent feature of modern societies not simply due to "self- and class interest, or of people's understandable tendency to view the political world from a limited standpoint", but because of how human reason works under "free institutions" (1993, 37).[2] Even when people use their reason to the best of their abilities, they will not come to agree on how human life should be lived. The disagreements that occur as a result are thus not unreasonable, and so, a society can be united around one and the same comprehensive doctrine only by means of oppressive use of state power (what Rawls refers to as "the fact of oppression", 1993, 37).

However, there may be more "general facts" than those listed by Rawls. One of them is that political decision-making in modern societies is dependent on a cognitive division of labor and needs to rely on different kinds of specialized knowledge (Kitcher 2011, 20 ff.). Also in this case, it is not only that modern-day policy-makers *de facto* tend to draw on advice from experts and expert bodies. Just as modern-day pluralism is not only a plain empirical fact (but also reasonable), our use of expertise does not only reflect how we in fact go about, but also what it is reasonable to do: under contemporary conditions of technical and societal complexity, the reliance on expert knowledge seems to be a condition for *good* political decision-making. In a range of questions, governments and citizens will not be able to make sound and well-founded political choices without consulting knowledgeable specialists. We will refer to this as *the fact of expertise* (Holst and Molander 2017; see also Münkler 2020, 12 ff, 37 ff.) and argue in what follows (and later in Chapter 3) that this fact has received far too little attention by political philosophers.

Still, by stating this, we obviously do not claim that better decision-making is guaranteed simply by consulting expertise. Even if the use of expertise is a condition for good government, expert knowledge may be limited and uncertain; experts may disagree, reasonably or not, and be biased and mistaken (see Chapter 4); and politicians may decide to put sound expert advice aside. This can be detrimental to, and even disastrous for, policy and decision quality. Yet, the most fundamental problem for democracy is – in Rawlsian terms – how the reliance on expertise can be made compatible with the idea of political power as "the power of citizens as a collective body" (Rawls 1993, 137). How to take advantage of expertise, while at the same time respecting citizens as free and equal persons having a sense of justice and the power of reason (Rawls 1993, 19)? When collectively binding decisions are based on knowledge and reasoning that are difficult to assess for non-experts, how then can they satisfy the legitimacy requirement of being reasonably endorsed by the citizens having to abide by them? How to judge the trustworthiness of expert judgments when you are not an expert yourself?

The social distribution of knowledge and epistemic trust

This fact of expertise – and the problem of experts that it triggers: how to judge the reliability of expert judgments as a non-expert – originates from the even more basic fact that knowledge is unevenly distributed in society. Still, it took some time before this attracted the attention of social scientists (Koppl 2018). One of the first to make the dispersed nature of knowledge a central problem for social theory was Friedrich von Hayek (Hayek 1937, 1945), with a focus on how knowledge and information is acquired by and distributed variably among market actors. When sociologist Alfred Schütz noted that "the social distribution of knowledge has not attracted the attention of social scientists that it merits" (Schütz 1953/1962, 15, n. 29a), he also mentioned Hayek as an exception.[3] Schütz' own essay "The well-informed citizen" was meant as a "modest step" in the direction of a theoretical inquiry into how knowledge is socially distributed (Schütz 1946/1964). Notably, Schütz distinguished this type of theoretical inquiry carefully from the branch of "sociology of knowledge", which "approached the problem ... merely from the angle of the ideological foundation of truth in its dependence upon social and especially, economic conditions, or from that of social implications of education, or that of the social role of the man of knowledge" (121). The topic of Schütz' interest was rather how "personal knowledge of each of us refers to the knowledge acquired by others – our teachers and predecessors – and handed down to us as a preorganized stock of problems" (121). The intricate question this socially derived character of our knowledge raises is "why do we believe in it?" (131).

Approaching the problem of knowledge distribution in society, Schütz constructed three ideal types: "the expert", "the man on the street" and "the well-informed citizen". The expert's knowledge is "restricted to a limited field but therein clear and distinct", and his opinions are based on "warranted assertions" (122). In contrast, the man on the street has vague knowledge of many fields that still is "*sufficiently* precise for practical purposes at hand" (122). He moreover follows "prescriptions as if they were a ritual", without questioning why they work. Finally, the well-informed citizen stands between the two other ideal types. This citizen does not possess, and does not aim at possessing, expert knowledge, but tries to "arrive at *reasonably founded* opinions in fields which he knows are at least mediately of concern to him although not bearing upon his purpose at hand" (122–123). Whereas it is enough for the man in the street to know that there are experts to consult, the well-informed citizen "considers himself perfectly qualified to decide who *is* a competent expert and even to make up his mind after having listened to opposing expert opinions" (123).

Placing his typology in the context of a democratic society, Schütz hoped that the opinions of the well-informed citizen would prevail over those of the man on the street (134). Still, he had little to say about the knowledge and capacities one must possess to reasonably consider oneself a "well-informed citizen" able to decide who is a true expert and to balance different expert opinions.

The problem of social distribution of knowledge was again raised by Berger and Luckman in *The Social Construction of Reality* (1966), where they pointed to the regression problem involved in the problem of judging who is an expert when you are not an expert yourself: what is needed is the "the prior advice of experts on experts" (Berger and Luckman 1966, 46), which again requires the prior advice of experts on experts on experts, etc. The social distribution of knowledge starting "with the simple fact that I do not know everything known to my fellowmen, and vice versa" then "culminates in exceedingly complex and esoteric systems of expertise" (Berger and Luckman 1966, 46). Later, Anthony Giddens in *The Consequences of Modernity* (1990) referred to "expert systems", "abstract" or "disembedded" systems of knowledge as "guarantees" that stabilize our expectations across time and space. As non-experts, we are therefore doomed to base our relations with experts on trust, and since we often lack the knowledge necessary to assess what experts do and the foundation of their "guarantees", this trust is close to "faith" (Giddens1990, 27).

Trust in experts, or epistemic trust, is a core topic in the field of social epistemology which has emerged during the past decades (see Goldman and Whitecomb 2011, Fricker et al. 2020). Traditionally, epistemology has focused on individual epistemic subjects and overlooked the social or intersubjective dimension of our knowledge. When John Locke famously listed reliance on authority *(argumentum ad verecundiam)* as one of the main sources of false beliefs (Locke [1690] 1997, § 19: 605), he did not take into account the fact that we as knowing subjects are dependent on the testimonies of others and frequently have to use "arguments from authority", for example, when appealing to expert opinion (Walton 1997). This means that not only direct evidence but also trust are sources of knowledge (Hardwig 1985, 1991). This is even more so with the increasing specialization of knowledge and epistemic division of labor.

Still, blind trust or deference to authority would seem to be irrational; there must be some justification for believing in an expert judgment. We must have good reasons to believe that the person we take to be an epistemic authority has good reasons for his judgment. But how can non-experts ascertain the trustworthiness or reliability of experts? A strategy would be to rely on *other* experts who can testify that there are good reasons to trust the expert's judgment (Hardwig 1991). This is to redistribute trust, in the sense that the object of trust is no longer the single expert but his or her co-experts (see Chapter 4), and, in the end, the expert community itself. The question then becomes what makes such a community trustworthy, and how to design trustworthy expert institutions (see Chapter 6).

The expertization of policy-making

Do current expert institutions deserve our trust? And if so, do we *de facto* trust them? In a time where autocratic populism is on the rise and with critiques of "elites" and "experts" from many corners, some claim that the faith in experts is rapidly fading. Rather, what we are witnessing is a growing distrust in science, "the death of expertise" (Nichols 2017), and post-truth politics. There is also a more optimistic version of this account, when it is claimed that the critique of science also has democratic promise (Jasanoff 2005), and that knowledge production has become more "socially distributed" (Gibbons et al. 1994) and "democratization of expertise" more widespread, replacing the previous dominance of professional expertise with more "pluralist" and "hybrid" forms (Krick 2015). From this perspective, a more radical questioning and even distrust in conventional expert authority may be a good thing.

Still, even under current conditions, citizens seem to accept "expertization" of policy-making in large doses and place considerable trust in procedures and institutions that privilege professional expertise and expert opinions. Illustratively, during corona times, trust in science and expert authorities increased in many countries (Gundersen et al. 2022), even as social inequalities and political cleavages were growing, and expert disagreements regarding the pandemic and how to respond to it were exposed in public debate on an almost daily basis. There are even signs of an increase in technocratic attitudes in some populations. In particular in the area of environmental policy, many people would prefer experts to be decision-makers, and not only advisors and executors (Bertsou 2022).

And indeed, many observers claim that the role and power of experts and expert knowledge is growing, and not fading (Turner 2003, Douglas 2009, Kitcher 2011, Münkler 2020): "Almost no relevant decision is made anymore without one or another form of expert advice being followed" (Münkler 2020, 22f.). This development is closely connected to what Frank Vibert (2007) refers to as "the rise of the unelected": the expanding role of courts, agencies, central banks and other expert bodies, which constitutes a new branch of government made up of those with expert knowledge, and that cuts across the traditional separation of powers (see also Olsen 2010). The myriad of scientific advisors, expert groups and public health institutes that were involved in the coronavirus response is only the latest example of this trend. Yet, we also see an increasing role for expert knowledge in contemporary politics among "the elected", as the share of parliamentarians and ministers with higher academic degrees has increased sharply, arguably turning democracy into a "diploma democracy" or "political meritocracy" (Bovens and Wille 2017). We will discuss the concrete manifestations of this "expertization" of governance in more detail in the next chapter.

Academic responses to expertization trends have always been mixed. The so-called technocracy thesis was, for instance, a topic of lively discussion among German philosophers and social scientists in the 1960s (see Rickert 1983). According to Helmut Schelsky (1961) and others, the more complex and technologically advanced a society is, the more politics is subjected to a *Sachzwang*, which removes issues from citizens' judgment to be left accessible only to technical experts. Critics of the thesis objected that the notion of technocracy camouflaged societal conflicts of interest and assumed that political issues either evaporated in a supposedly de-ideologized techno-scientific civilization or could be transformed into technical issues. As one of these critics, Jürgen Habermas took the *Verwissenschaftlichung* (scientization) of politics as a contemporary fact, and inspired by John Dewey, he outlined a "pragmatic" model of the relationship between science and politics. He contrasted this model with the "technocratic" model of the replacement of politics and with a "decisionistic" model which made a sharp distinction between facts and values, means and ends, and entrusted science the role to inform about facts and suggest alternative means, while it was the role of politicians to decide on goals and thus take a stand in the endless struggle between different value systems. According to the "pragmatic" model, it is not possible to clearly distinguish purely technical aspects of political questions, and the model envisions a mutual exchange between democratic opinion formation and scientific inquiry (Habermas 1968). However, while attractive, this model raises a range of problems concerning the responsibilities of the expert role and the accountability of experts (Münkler 2020, 180), which will be discussed in the chapters to come.

The current expertization of political life and public decision-making has given rise to similar controversies. For example, proponents of evidence-based or evidence-informed policy-making see a larger role for expertise and evidence as leading to better policies (Davies et al. 2000, Head 2015, Parkhurst 2017). But also political philosophers are concerned with how the use of expertise can improve political decision-making. There are those who want more expert rule because voters are largely ignorant (Brennan 2016); others try, as Habermas did in the 1960s, to figure out how expertise can contribute to rather than replace democratic deliberation and decision-making (see also Kitcher 2011, Christiano 2012, Moore 2017). Still others are deeply critical and diagnose our contemporary form of rule with experts as a threat to democracy under headings as "technocracy" (Meynaud 1968, Fischer 1990), "expertization" (Turner 2003), "post-democracy", (Crouch 2004), "façade democracy" (Streeck 2014) or "epistemization of the political" (Bogner 2021).

In Chapter 3, we will take a closer look at the controversies over the role of expertise in democracies. But what is this thing – *expertise* – that some welcome and others fear? In order to get a grip on this, we must first clarify what it means to be an expert and who the experts are.

What is an expert?

We have already talked about expertise in terms of "specialized knowledge", and this clearly captures something essential. In an influential exercise, philosopher Alvin Goldman (2001/2011, 114) defines experts as those who "have more beliefs (or high degrees of belief) in true propositions and/or fewer beliefs in false propositions within a domain than most people do (or better: than the vast majority of people do)". From this definition, we learn that experts are exactly "domain" specialists, but also that expertise is relative: experts in, say, quantum physics or labor market economics know more about quantum physics or labor market economics than the rest of us. However, there must also be a threshold. In Goldman's (2011, 115) words, to qualify as an expert, "a person must possess a substantial body of truths". If someone knows more about trivial aspects of something or has some sketchy knowledge about something that we all are mostly ignorant about, we would be hesitant to call this person an expert. If someone knows a lot about EU politicians' tastes in music and food, but apart from this lacks any extra insights in how the EU works, she would not deserve the name of an EU expert.

In addition, according to Goldman (2011, 115), experts possess not only accurate information, but also "a capacity to deploy or exploit this fund of information to form beliefs in true answers to new questions that may be posed in the domain". Real experts understand and internalize their knowledge in ways that make it possible for them to apply it to new intellectual and practical problems in their field. A true expert in literary theory will be able to utilize and develop this stock of theory when a new kind of poetry or novel appears; an expert engineer will be able to build safe bridges in new landscapes.

Finally, adding to Goldman, expert knowledge is knowledge that is of interest to someone and called for by someone. Experts are mandated (Gundersen 2018). The status of knowledgeable persons as experts is based on a certain social recognition: their knowledge must be considered significant and relevant, and their guidance asked for. Hence, experts are not only knowers within some domain, they also communicate with non-experts outside of this domain, who ask for information, assessments, advice and recommendations (Stehr and Grundmann 2010, Lane 2014,

Hirschi 2018, 29–30). Proper experts are therefore expected to be able to translate their expert knowledge, as far as possible, into vocabularies that outsiders may be able to understand, and to speak on the basis of their expertise (and nothing else).

Expertise and science

Another shorthand definition of expertise that we have used in our discussions so far is that of "professional", "academic" or "scientific" knowledge. Initially, this is sensible: there is a special relationship between expertise and science, since what standardly counts as the most authoritative type of knowledge in modern societies is that which is validated, or regarded as validated, according to scientific norms and procedures. Accordingly, you often see the categories "scientist" and "expert" used interchangeably, and expert committees and other expert bodies are often crowded with scientists and professionals with disciplinary background from medicine, engineering, economics, etc.

What counts as scientific knowledge can of course be defined more or less strictly. Among the proponents of evidence-based policy-making, the hardliners restrict "scientific evidence" to results deriving from research based on rigorous methodologies – particularly experimental studies organized as randomized controlled trials (RCTs) – and synthesized in systematic reviews (Head 2015, 473). In softer, and we believe sounder, versions of the argument, evidence also includes other forms of research (e.g. qualitative research) and even informal evidence such as clinical expertise (Oliver et al. 2014, 3).

Moreover, even if proper experts are expected to operate according to, or at least in ways that do not contradict, scientific standards, they are not necessarily full members of scientific communities. For instance, the typical expert in the European Commission expert group system is not a professor, but a national civil servant with a higher academic degree. Ministries can be crowded with lawyers, economists and other experts who do not take an active part in academic publishing.

There are, moreover, sources of expertise other than scientific training, such as especially relevant practical experiences: experts can have come to know a lot about something by means of practical engagement with certain issues over time (Collins and Evans 2007). When experienced civil servants so often serve as experts in public policy-making, it is due to their practically gained regulatory expertise, adding to their expertise acquired through disciplinary competence. Civil society actors and interest group representatives often also contribute practical field knowledge, not seldom combined with academic competence.

Policy-making also allows for, and frequently needs, some would say, input from non-professionals with first-hand experiential knowledge on the issue at hand. Particularly work in science and technology studies (STS) has challenged the idea that only scientists and academics can provide knowledge relevant to policy-making. Citizens and other stakeholders may also possess useful knowledge, which is based on practical experience and opinions (Wynne 1996, Callon 1999). We see this, for example, within health and social policy where users of public services are included in policy formulation and implementation processes as "lay experts" or "experts-by-experience" (Krick 2015). This broad notion of expertise can be apt for some analytical purposes (see, e.g. Pedersen, Holst and Fjell 2021 on drug policy), but focusing on all kinds of knowledge providers in policy-making can also throw the net too wide. The challenge of an increasing role of experts and of an expanding expert rule, for instance, refers specifically to political actors and knowledge bearers with academic degrees and credentials, and not to all kinds of "knowers".

Lastly, an important distinction can be drawn between the ability to "contribute" in a domain of expertise ("contributory expertise") and having enough competence in this domain to be able to make sense of what its contributory experts are saying and doing ("interactional expertise") (Collins and Evans 2007, 13–44). The latter is vital for the communication between different types of expertise and between experts and non-experts, and so ultimately for the fulfilment of experts' mandate and legitimate expectations among those who ask for expert advice. An "interactional expert" can be, for example, the broadly oriented professor with the ability to deliberate with academic experts across fields and disciplines, or the stakeholder expert who serves as "knowledge broker" and bridges lay and professional perspectives (Meyer 2010).

With all of this granted, we allow ourselves to focus in this book on the role of academic, scientific or professional expertise. We do this because in many cases, also in policy-making contexts, such expertise represents the best validated knowledge, and the most proper expertise – the knowledge most worthy of being given the special status of expertise. It is also typically this type of expertise commentators have in mind when they diagnose modern societies as "expertized" or discuss whether an increasing role of experts and expert knowledge in decision-making is desirable. Moreover, as we will see in Chapter 2, this focus is in line with how expertise in policy-making is approached within most empirical research in political and social science.

Moral expertise

Finally, to settle our notion of "expert" and "expertise", we have to address the relationship between expert knowledge and normative issues. Because, to be sure, political decisions do not only involve questions of facts and means efficiency: what is the state of affairs? Will this or the other policy work? Politics also concerns questions of what is right and good: is the state of affairs as we would like it to be, and if not, on what basis do we make our judgment? Policies can be deemed effective, or not so effective, but according to which standards and parameters?

Few will deny this, but it triggers some intricate questions. For one thing, is it possible to separate is- and ought issues in political affairs, or are facts rather inseparably intertwined with moral and ethical considerations? Here, we must first distinguish between logical and empirical levels. On a logical level, issues of "is" and "ought" are of different kinds. Descriptive and causal characteristics – questions of how things are, of why things are as they are, and of whether and how an intervention (e.g. the introduction of a new policy) has effects – are logically independent of questions of whether things ought to be like they are, how one ought to intervene and how one should assess the effects of an intervention. One cannot infer what one ought to do from facts alone. Hence, in principle, is- and ought questions can be kept apart.

Yet, in actual policy-making, it is often hard to distinguish neatly between is- and ought issues, and no less so when expert communities and bodies are included. Parkhurst (2017) mentions the example of the American Medical Association (AMA), which argued that US abortion policy needed to be "evidence-based", thus ignoring that the question of abortion for many people is a question of values rather than of facts. That "is" and "ought" are difficult to keep apart should come as no surprise if we consider recent arguments in philosophy of science against the ideal of "value free inquiry", for instance, arguments about reliance on "value-laden concepts" or more recent arguments about the necessity of value judgments to set the evidential standards for accepting a hypothesis when there is a risk for error (Rudner 1953, Putnam 2002, Dupré 2007, Douglas 2009, Kitcher 2011, Alexandrova 2017; see also Rolin 2020, Gundersen 2022). That "is" and "ought" in practice often shade into each other is also illustrated by theories of policy expertise in political science, such as Haas' (1992) notion of "epistemic communities", which he defines as communities that share causal and normative beliefs and ideas about policy solutions.

Anyone acquainted with the expert reports of real-world policy-making will also have learnt that such reports seldom respect any strict demarcation between facts and values. For instance, the terms of reference of many government-appointed expert groups may look purely technical, asking for "evidence", "mappings", "descriptions", "comparisons", "explanations" and/or "forecasts" (see Renn 2022 on "the analytical function of science advice"). Still, even groups that work on such seemingly "value free" mandates, and that are not asked to provide policy recommendations, tend to deliver reports that also refer to ethical and political values that are interpreted and ranked more or less explicitly. For instance, they will typically define concerns such as "sustainability", "subsidiarity", "inclusion", "social cohesion" and "individual rights", and balance and prioritize such concerns when they come into conflict. Also, very often, some policies will be preferred over others.

At the same time, in most policy-making, we would come a long way by distinguishing factual from evaluative questions despite uncertainties and hard cases. Studies indicate that a commitment to keep "is" and "ought" apart in deliberations, for example, by means of sequencing knowledge issues from policy issues, guides scientific experts' involvement in policy-making (Tellmann 2016, Holst and Molander 2017, Gundersen 2018). Esteemed science advice arrangements are also often set up with this separation in mind, including the Science Advice Mechanism of the EU. To be sure, estimations of effects of policies, or within policy domains, are impossible without normative standards – effects must be assessed on or for something – but once such standards have been settled, interpreted and operationalized, measuring effects can be regarded as a relatively technical question.

However, expert groups and bodies are also often asked quite explicitly to give advice regarding the operationalization and balancing of normative concerns and values. For instance, if we examine the European Central Bank's (ECB) mission statement, its main objective is "the maintenance of price stability", and the ECB is given discretion to define "price stability for the common good", distinguished from price stability that is less "sound", and to interpret what it implies to show "due regard" to principles such as "independence", "decentralization", "accountability" and "equal treatment".[4] Similarly, the mandates of European Commission expert groups often rather explicitly ask for judgments on distributive and other normative issues. In effect, this is to recognize experts' authority also on questions that involve moral considerations. Recent decades have also seen the emergence of a new class of "ethics experts" or "bioethics experts" hailing from the life sciences, philosophy, law or even theology, who provide ethical advice to numerous governments and international organizations – although their actual contribution to more morally informed policy-making is contested (Littoz-Monnet 2020).

To claim that there at all can be such a thing as moral experts proper is obviously controversial. The default position in democratic theory seems to be that there cannot. According to Robert Dahl (1989, 66), there is no moral knowledge, and hence no moral expertise, because there are no methods for demonstrating the intersubjective validity of moral judgments. Nevertheless, he admits that moral questions cannot be reduced to "subjective" questions of "taste"; there is scope for "argument drawing on human reason and human experience" (Dahl 1989, 67). This opens up for the existence of moral expertise after all, in the sense that this seems to follow, in principle, from all accounts that consider normative questions to be possible objects of rational discourse (Gesang 2010; see also Hoffman 2012): if some moral arguments are more qualified, better justified, than others then there may also be some persons who are better at making well-founded moral arguments than others.

This granted, one could think of moral expertise in the following way:

> Someone familiar with moral concepts and with moral arguments, who has ample time to gather information and think about it, may reasonably be expected to reach a soundly based conclusion more often than someone who is unfamiliar with moral concepts and moral arguments and has little time.
>
> (Singer 1972, 117; see also Gesang 2010, Rinderle 2014, 35)

In addition to this competence in normative analysis, moral experts should arguably have competences that, to a certain extent, overlap with scientific expertise because they have to reason on the basis of relevant facts and take scientific theories in the relevant domain into account (Hoffman 2012). In real-world policy-making, one could find experts with the combination of these competences, for instance, among ethicists with an applied orientation, but also in epistemic communities connected to particular policy domains where members have training in normative theory and argumentation.

Furthermore, one could think of a moral expert as someone who contributes to political deliberation by clarifying what is at stake. A moral expert may conceptualize and elaborate on the meaning of involved norms, values and ends; explicate the implications of pursuing this or that end or of defining this or that value in one way or another; explore normative conflicts; and so on. All of this would actually be compatible with what Max Weber referred to as "value freedom": the critical functions of science include not only clarifying the relationship between ends and means and the possible side effects of the choice of certain means, but also a "dialetical" critique, that is, "a testing of the ideals according to the postulate of internal *consistency* of the desired end" (Weber 1904/1949, 54). In this way, the critique could "aid the acting willing person in attaining self-clarification concerning the final axioms from which his desired ends are derived" (54).

But moral experts may also go beyond such clarifying tasks and act as "legislators", justifying norms and political aims and arguing for priorities and ways of balancing normative ideas and ideals. They may defend this or that as the appropriate metric of distributive justice and then suggest a principle of just distribution – for example, of healthcare – or state this or that as the reasonable way to approach a conflict between rights.

We have argued that expertise reliance or dependency is a fact of contemporary political life in the sense that is hard to see how well-functioning modern democracies can do without expert knowledge and expert arrangements. But at the same time, there is a worry that expert dependency may undermine political equality – a worry that increases the more experts do not just act as purely technical experts but enter "the Kingdom of Ends". However, normative political theory has so far been less concerned with the "fact of expertise" than with the "the fact of reasonable pluralism" and has surprisingly little to say about the proper use of expert knowledge in democracies, compared to the extensive discussions of, for example, the relations between democracy and the rule of law.

In this book, we contend that a normative discussion of the role of expertise in democracy is crucial both for scholarship and practice, and that such a discussion needs to be anchored in what we know about actual patterns of expert involvement in policy-making. In the next chapter, we therefore draw on a wide range of empirical research on expertise and policy-making to discuss the expertization of contemporary policy-making and the many channels through which expert knowledge is currently included in policy-making in democratic systems, before we turn to theories of democracy in Chapter 3.

Notes

1 Just as the political philosopher must take this into account by limiting her theorizing to non-comprehensive or "free-standing" considerations about fair terms for cooperation among citizens (Rawls 1993, IV:§5). Charles Larmore has argued that what distinguishes political philosophy from moral philosophy is that it reflects on the conditions for legitimate use of coercive state power given the fact of reasonable pluralism (Larmore 2020). Philosophers, like all others, may of course also theorize on the basis of a comprehensive doctrine and contribute to both scholarly debates and democratic deliberations. Yet, when doing so in the role as "moral experts" (see below and Chapter 4), they should not be attributed general authority (Viehoff 2016), but authority as qualified spokespersons for views that are endorsed only by some citizens.
2 See Rawls on "the burdens of judgement" (1993, Lecture 2, §2).
3 See Koppl (2018) on the connection between Hayek and Schütz, who both participated in Ludwig von Mises' seminar in Vienna in the 1920s. On the relation between Austrian economics and Schütz' phenomenological sociology, see Prendergast (1986).
4 www.ecb.europa.eu/ecb/orga/escb/html/index.en.html

2 Expertise in policy-making

What role do experts and expert knowledge actually play in policy-making in modern democracies? While the topic is one of long-standing interest in the social sciences, recent decades have seen a multiplication of academic efforts to describe and explain the involvement of experts in policy-making. This has been driven on the one hand by critical scholarly interest in what many see as the increasing power of experts in decision-making, and on the other hand by the movement for more evidence-based policy-making that has gained traction both in policy circles and in the research community. Empirical scholarship on expertise stretches across various sub-disciplines of political science and sociology. It includes public policy and administration research on evidence-based policy-making, knowledge utilization and policy advisory systems, work in international relations on epistemic communities, and comparative political economy research on ideas and politics, as well as sociological work on professions and knowledge, and science and technology studies (see Christensen 2021 for an overview).

Levels and drivers of expertization

These empirical literatures examine the role of expertise in policy-making at different levels of analysis. Some literatures focus on the expert knowledge or evidence itself (Head 2015) or on the ideas held by experts (Campbell 2002). In other literatures, the expert or the community of experts – that is, the profession (Abbott 1988, Fourcade 2006) or the "epistemic community" (Haas 1992) – is at the center of the action. Other work again zooms out to the entire system of institutions producing knowledge and advice, that is, the "knowledge regime" (Campbell and Pedersen 2014), the "policy advisory system" (Craft and Halligan 2017) or the broader nexus of culture, politics and institutions (for instance, Jasanoff 2005 on "civic epistemologies").

DOI: 10.4324/9781003106555-3

These literatures also use different concepts to capture the role of experts and their knowledge in policy-making, which are not without normative content. The literature on evidence-based policy-making speaks of how evidence "informs" policy-making and of the "uptake", "use" or "utilization" of expert knowledge (Oliver et al. 2014, Head 2015, Parkhurst 2017). By contrast, work on epistemic communities, professions, and ideas and politics is more likely to talk about how experts and their knowledge "influence" public policies (Haas 1992, Campbell and Pedersen 2014; see Christensen 2021).

At the same time, there is broad consensus across these literatures about the basic reasons why decision-makers draw on expert knowledge when designing policies. Most fundamentally, decision-makers need expertise to make sense of the challenges they face and to formulate policy responses to these problems (Béland and Cox 2010). Experts may help identify cause-and-effect relationships and give advice on the likely results of different actions, frame an issue and define policy alternatives, and design concrete policies (Haas 1992). The need for expert advice has become more pressing with the growing specialization and complexity of society. These conditions confront decision-makers with growing uncertainty: they need to make choices without adequate information about the situation or about the expected outcomes of different actions (Haas 1992).

Yet, it is also widely agreed that decision-makers seek the knowledge of experts not only out of a genuine need to solve policy problems, but also symbolically to bolster legitimacy. With the high value placed on science and rationality in modern society, it has become increasingly important to show that policy-making draws on experts and expert knowledge, since this creates an appearance that decisions are made in a fact-based and impartial way (Weiss 1979, Feldman and March 1981, Markoff and Montecinos 1993, Boswell 2008). Citizens, opposition parties and interest groups may be more willing to accept policy solutions that are based on expert knowledge than on ideology or interests.

These twin trends – the greater need for specialized expertise to solve problems in increasingly complex societies and the mounting pressure to show that policy-making is rational by relying on experts – form the backdrop for the expertization trend that we see today. In the rest of this chapter, we will provide an overview of the manifold channels, mechanisms and arrangements through which expert knowledge is incorporated into political decision-making in contemporary democracies. We will also discuss how the involvement of experts in policy-making varies across countries and key international organizations, showing how expertization is not uniform but rather that there is considerable variation within this broad trend.

Expert arrangements

Expertization comes in many shapes and variants, and contemporary governance systems offer a wide array of channels for supplying expert knowledge to political decision-makers, ranging from expertise in ministries and agencies, via various forms of advisory bodies, to think tanks and consultancies. Significantly, the specific institutions for providing expert advice to decision-makers vary across countries, policy areas and governance levels (Campbell and Pedersen 2014, Craft and Halligan 2017, Christensen and Holst 2021, Christensen and Gornitzka 2022). In the following, we will take a closer look at the range of different institutions that provide decision-makers with expert knowledge, and offer some observations about how expert arrangements vary between different political systems.

Expertise in the bureaucracy

A natural place to start is the executive branch and, more specifically, the permanent government administration. In modern democracies, elected leaders have at their disposal a sprawling bureaucracy divided into departments, division and units with specialized tasks and often considerable specialized expertise. This bureaucracy is a major and proximate provider of expert knowledge to political leaders. Politicians' reliance on the bureaucracy for expertise was not lost on Max Weber, who famously observed: "The 'political master' always finds himself, vis-à-vis the trained official, in the position of a 'dilettante' facing the expert" (Weber 1922/1978, 991). Indeed, the superior expertise of the bureaucracy is one of the main reasons why elected leaders delegate great responsibilities to unelected administrative bodies, and a principal source of the influence of these bodies over public policies.

Expertise plays a somewhat different role within different types of administrative bodies. *Policy bureaucracies*, such as national ministries and the secretariats of international organizations, have as their task to develop and run policy programs and to provide policy advice to politicians (Page and Jenkins 2005). These bureaucracies are in direct contact with political leaders and are expected to be responsive to the goals and wishes of politicians (though more so in national bureaucracies than in international ones). At the same time, bureaucrats draw on expert knowledge to formulate policies and advice, which is acquired through both academic training and experience on the job. For instance, a bureaucrat in a finance ministry may advice politicians about the likely effects of a proposed tax reform, based on her academic training in economics and her experience with the administrative challenges posed by the existing tax regime.

However, the type of expertise offered by policy bureaucracies varies greatly across countries (Page and Wright 1999, Christensen 2017, Peters 2018). In some countries, such as Germany and the Scandinavian states, bureaucrats often provide specialist competences in law, economics or other disciplines. In countries such as the United Kingdom and Ireland, bureaucrats are often generalists: they have an academic background unrelated to their tasks and provide advice based on knowledge acquired on the job. In France, most top bureaucrats have a dedicated civil service education from a *grande école* covering political science, law and economics. We see the same kind of variation at the international level: the European Commission mainly seeks generalists who are capable of handling any policy dossier, whereas the International Monetary Fund mostly recruits economists with PhDs from leading US universities to its staff (Chwieroth 2010, Christensen 2015).

Especially in places where bureaucratic recruitment is based on specialized skills, policy bureaucracies constitute an important channel for incorporating academic insights in decision-making. Academic knowledge flows into the bureaucracy through new recruits who bring what they learned in university to their jobs in a ministry (Christensen 2017). And given the proximity of policy bureaucracies to political leaders, their expertise may have a considerable impact on the content of public policies.

Ministries sometimes also have dedicated research units. For instance, most German ministries have one or more research units with a large expert staff that conduct relatively advanced research (Campbell and Pedersen 2014). In addition, some countries have dedicated scientific advisers in the bureaucracy, who have a special responsibility for providing advice and promoting the use of science and evidence in government. Most notably, the United Kingdom has Chief Scientific Advisers in most government departments as well as an overarching Government Chief Scientific Adviser (Bressers et al. 2017). During the coronavirus crisis, Chief Scientific Adviser Sir Patrick Vallance, a former professor of medicine and research director for a large pharmaceutical company, played a central role in the government's pandemic response. The European Commission has set up a similar system, with a group of seven independent Chief Scientific Advisers and a larger consortium of experts from different fields who provide scientific input to the Commission.

While policy bureaucracies develop policies, the implementation of these policies and the regulation of different sectors of the economy have increasingly been delegated to a different kind of bureaucratic body, namely *agencies*. Agencies are deliberately located at an arm's length from political leaders and thus enjoy greater independence than ministries. This reflects the fact that agencies usually have more specialized and technical tasks (Schrefler 2010). For instance, the European Medicines Agency (EMA) is in charge of assessing the safety and effectiveness of vaccines in the EU, among other things. Food safety authorities are responsible for controlling that foodstuffs do not contain chemicals that are harmful to people's health, and competition authorities analyze, for instance, whether companies abuse a dominant market position or whether a merger will hurt competition in a specific market.

The work of many agencies thus involves detailed technical research and assessments requiring highly specialized knowledge in medicine, chemistry, engineering, biology, economics and so on. In some agencies, research is even the main or one of the main activities of the organization, such as in the Norwegian Institute of Public Health or Institute of Marine Research or in Italian government research institutes (Galanti and Lippi 2022). For that reason, the scientific expertise and analytical capacity of agencies are a fundamental element of the operations of agencies, and key to their legitimacy, reputation and autonomy (Majone 1996, Carpenter 2010). This is the case both for national agencies and for agencies at the international level, such as the rapidly growing number of EU agencies (Busuioc and Rimkute 2020). In other words, through the work of agencies, scientific knowledge has a profound impact on the many regulations that characterize modern societies, including air safety, environmental risks or health and safety standards in the workplace.

A related type of government body where experts enjoy even greater independence is *central banks*. In most countries, independent central banks have been delegated the responsibility for setting monetary policy as well as significant regulatory functions (McPhilemy and Moschella 2019). Based on the idea that the setting of the interest rate should not be influenced by the short-term electoral concerns of politicians, central banks have been insulated from political control. The role of politicians has been limited to defining the overarching goals of monetary policies, primarily the aim of low inflation as expressed in inflation targets. Beyond that, there has been a growing consensus that the decisions of central banks should be based primarily on objective economic expertise and analysis. Central banks have thus become "scientized" over time (Marcussen 2006). Central banks have expanded their staff of highly trained economists, and many have established research departments and close links to academia. This is not only the case for national central banks. The European Central Bank has emerged as one of the most independent and expertise-minded central banks, with the power to set monetary policies for the entire Eurozone (Jabko 2003). In other words, central banks are one of the most blatant examples of the expertization of decision-making in contemporary democracies.

Expertise in courts

Similarly, the power to interpret and apply laws is delegated to legal experts. As opposed to the bureaucratic experts discussed earlier, judges are located in a separate branch of power: the judicial branch. Judges in most developed countries thus operate independently of political leaders, although there of course are cases where politicians seek to influence the courts through appointments, such as in the United States or in Poland. Whereas legislators make the laws, the courts define how these laws should be interpreted and applied, for instance, when the law is too general or unclear or when different laws contradict each other. And judges make these decisions based on the legal knowledge they have acquired through university training in law and their experience from the legal system.

The power of the courts has increased in recent decades as a result of the expansion and specification of legal regulations, a process referred to as juridification (Blichner and Molander 2008). The most striking example is the growing role of international courts (see Føllesdal and Ulfstein 2018), from the European Court of Justice and the European Court of Human Rights, to international criminal courts and tribunals of trade settlements. Some of these international courts have a wide portfolio and make binding decisions on everything from the posting of workers via gender quotas to environmental regulation and cultural policy. Others are more specialized, such as the World Trade Organization's Appellate Body, the International Centre for Settlement of Investment Disputes and The Tribunal of the Law of the Sea, and recruit court judges with advanced and sometimes highly specialized academic training. In addition, the size of courts' secretariats of legal experts has expanded rapidly, in parallel with the increasing role of dispute settlements through courts and the growing technical and regulatory complexity of court cases. In short, in recent years, a whole range of policy decisions have effectively been moved from elected leaders to unelected legal expert bodies.

Parliamentary research bodies

In addition to the expertise located within the executive and judicial branch, the legislative branch may be able to draw on separate expert capacities (Akerlof et al. 2019). In some systems, there are dedicated research and analysis bodies connected to parliament. These bodies serve to bolster the ability of parliament to make well-informed decisions and to strengthen the position of lawmakers relative to the government by reducing the executive's advantage in terms of expertise and analytical capacities. The most prominent example is the United States, where Congress can draw on public policy research and evaluations and budget analyses produced by the Congressional Research Service, the Congressional Budget Office and the Government Accountability Office, which all have significant research capacities (Campbell and Pedersen 2014). The German Bundestag has a research service (*Wissenschaftliche Dienste*), and the UK Parliament has a Parliamentary Office for Science and Technology (POST), among other mechanisms for drawing on expert knowledge (Geddes 2021). But also the European Parliament has established an in-house research body with considerable capacity – the European Parliamentary Research Service – which provides analysis and research on European policy issues. However, in many other systems, parliament has very limited independent research and analysis capacities at its disposal.

Government-appointed advisory bodies

In addition to expertise provided by the government bureaucracy proper, politicians rely on a wide variety of government-established advisory bodies, such as advisory councils, scientific panels, commissions, task forces and expert groups (Bressers et al. 2017). These are consultative bodies with the task of providing government with analysis, knowledge and policy recommendations. Such bodies are typically appointed and funded by government but include outside experts, such as university professors. Advisory bodies typically gather, synthesize and draw out the policy implications of scientific research, but seldom carry out extensive research on their own (although there are exceptions). While some advisory bodies enjoy great independence, these kinds of bodies may also be subject to significant *de facto* political and bureaucratic control (Hesstvedt and Christensen 2021).

Advisory bodies may be permanent or temporary and are found both at the national and international level. A prominent example of a permanent body is the United Nations' Intergovernmental Panel on Climate Change (IPCC), whose task is to provide objective scientific information on human-induced climate change, its consequences and possible policy responses. Councils of economic advisors are another example: such councils are found, for instance, in the United States, Germany, France and Denmark. These councils are usually made up of prominent university professors in economics and a permanent expert staff, and provide analysis and policy advice to government on economic issues (Campbell and Pedersen 2014). (Tellingly, the professors on the Danish economic council are known simply as the "wise men".) Some countries rely heavily on permanent advice bodies. For instance, the Netherlands has several sector-specific advisory councils, including for foreign policy and culture, and a cross-cutting body providing advice on issues with major social and political consequences – the Netherlands Scientific Council for Government Policy (WRR) (Bressers et al. 2017).

Other countries instead make extensive use of temporary advisory bodies to examine specific policy problems and recommend solutions. For instance, the Scandinavian countries have long traditions for appointing *ad hoc* advisory commissions (a.k.a. commissions of inquiry or public committees) as a first stage in the development of policy to address major societal issues (Christensen and Holst 2017, Dahlström et al. 2021, Hesstvedt and Christiansen 2022). These commissions often have mixed membership – that is, some mix of bureaucrats, interests groups, academics and sometimes also politicians – and provide recommendations that can carry considerable weight in the policy-making process. Similarly, the European Commission has an extensive system of expert groups (including both permanent and temporary groups), which provide specialist advice to supplement the Commission's in-house expertise (Gornitzka and Sverdrup 2011). These expert groups are typically made up of some combination of national officials, interest group representatives and academics.

Decision-makers' reliance on advisory bodies was on display during the coronavirus crisis, with scientific councils and task forces being established or activated in nearly every jurisdiction to provide scientific advice regarding all aspects of the coronavirus response. For instance, the United Kingdom activated its Scientific Advisory Group for Emergencies (SAGE) to advise on the coronavirus responses. SAGE brought together experts from government, academia and industry and bundled advice from a number of connected expert groups on more specific topics, such as genome sequencing or behavioral science insights about how people adhere to coronavirus measures. In Belgium, a series of temporary scientific expert groups were set up to advice cabinet on coronavirus measures, with participation from prominent university professors in epidemiology and virology as well as health economics and motivational psychology. Advisory bodies were also appointed to look beyond the pandemic. For instance, in France, President Macron appointed an expert commission made up of 26 leading economists (including three Nobel Prize winners) to examine the long-term economic challenges related to climate change, inequality and ageing. In other words, the multitude of advisory bodies that we find in modern democracies are important institutional channels for linking science and policy – both during crisis and in regular times.

External knowledge providers

Of course, political decision-makers also rely on expert advice from organizations outside of government. In fact, one of the most important trends over the past decades is the "externalization" of policy advice, meaning that politicians rely less exclusively on internal advice from bureaucrats and instead turn toward a variety of external actors for advice (Craft and Howlett 2013). In many countries, the field of external providers of policy-relevant knowledge has expanded dramatically in recent decades, including a growing number of "new" advisory actors such as think tanks and consultancies.

Yet, also more established types of external knowledge-providing organizations remain important. *Universities* are important producers of both experts and expertise for policy-making. Not only do universities produce the graduates in economics, law, etc. that go on to serve as bureaucratic advisors in government and international organizations; university professors are also frequent participants in government-appointed scientific councils, advisory commissions and expert groups (Christensen and Holst 2017). Studies have also shown that university research is one important source of information for government policy-makers, even if the use of academic research by politicians and bureaucrats varies considerably (Head et al. 2014, Newman et al. 2016). The mechanisms through which university research can reach policy-making are manifold. They range from the more institutionalized mechanisms discussed earlier to when a specific piece of research influences media debate and thereby the political agenda or when politicians or bureaucrats informally seek advice directly from academics they know and trust.

Academics not only give expert advice to political decision-makers, they sometimes also take on the role of *public intellectuals* (Posner 2002) addressing the general public on questions of political relevance. Public intellectuals do not only popularize their own work but go beyond their academic specialisms and contribute to public controversies on questions of a principled character. Many distinguished academics have taken this role, including figures such as the Nobel Prize laureates in economics Friedrich von Hayek, Gunnar Myrdal, Milton Friedman and Amartya Sen, and philosophers such as Hannah Arendt, Jürgen Habermas and Martha Nussbaum. However, the influential political philosopher John Rawls hardly commented at all publicly on current political affairs. An opposite example is Noam Chomsky whose writings on American foreign policy and capitalism have no connection with his groundbreaking work in linguistics.

Independent *research institutes* may also play a significant role as providers of policy-relevant knowledge. While some research institutes are focused on basic research (e.g. some of the German Max Planck Institutes), there is also a broad array of applied research institutes that conduct commissioned research for government and other clients. For instance, Norway has a large sector of social-scientific research institutes that study issues related to the welfare state, the labor market and immigration, among other things. These institutes frequently conduct studies for ministries, agencies or local governments – for example, an evaluation of an integration program for immigrants – providing a direct link to policy-making.

Alongside these established institutions, *think tanks* have emerged as a new form of external knowledge provider in recent decades. Note that the broadest definitions of think tanks include many research institutes as well (e.g. McGann 2020). More narrowly understood, think tanks are organizations that actively seek to influence the policy-making process based on expertise and analysis (Rich 2004). At the very least, this means that think tanks are more oriented toward current policy debates and more accessible publications aimed at policy-makers than universities and research institutes. At the most, it means that think tanks advocate ideological or partisan goals (Weaver 1989). Think tanks of the latter kind may contribute to enlightenment of public debates, but are partisan, and offer knowledge that to a greater or lesser extent is selected and framed based on political-ideological criteria (Christensen and Holst 2020). In the words of Hayek, they act as "secondhand dealers of ideas" (Hayek 1949). Of course, this can make their advice more relevant and palatable for political leaders than knowledge supplied by traditional actors. Think tanks of the former kind typically have stronger scholarly credentials, for instance, through in-house research capacity or links to academics.

Though originally an American phenomenon, think tanks have been gaining ground in many other countries in recent years, although their strength and impact differ. For instance, in Brussels, a plethora of think tanks have sprung up to provide the EU institutions with politically relevant advice, many of them relatively scholarly in their approach – such as the Center for European Policy Studies and the European Policy Centre (Kelstrup 2018).

Consultancy firms have also become increasingly important suppliers of policy analysis, evaluations and advice to government. Government makes use of external policy consultants for several reasons, including the need for skills and expertise not present within the permanent bureaucracy (sometimes as a result of cutbacks in in-house capacities) and the desire to bring in "fresh" outside perspectives that can stimulate change in organizations and policies (Howlett and Migone 2013). Consultants usually have higher education, for instance, within fields such as economics, business administration or political science. The role of policy consultants is usually to repackage data and information but can also involve more extensive data collection and analysis (Van den Berg et al. 2020). For instance, consultancies carry out a large number of ex ante and ex post policy evaluations for governments and international organizations, which involve appraising the effects of a policy proposal or an existing policy (Højlund 2015).

While the expertise provided by external consultants in some cases may be similar to that offered by bureaucrats, it is often argued that consultants rely on generic management and organization models drawn from the private sector in their advice. Policy consultants also differ in important ways from external academic advisers: consultants are not committed to scientific norms of independence and objectivity but rather see themselves as providing services to a client. Relying on consultants rather than academics for expert input may therefore make it easier for government to control what kind of advice they receive, since they as client can make sure that commissioned reports avoid sensitive topics and unwanted advice (e.g. De Francesco 2018).

Adding to this, political leaders may draw on expert advice from *interest groups and private companies*. These actors of course seek to advocate specific interests or aims, such as business interests, consumer interests or environmental protection. However, to gain access to policy-makers, interest groups also need to offer relevant knowledge to politicians and bureaucrats, for instance, about the economic conditions in a specific sector (Bouwen 2002). Sometimes policy-makers are completely dependent on the knowledge provided by companies, for instance, when it comes to regulating new technologies that only the companies working with the technology fully grasp, such as nanotechnology (Moos 2014). Growing expectations that public policies should be based on evidence may also have forced interest groups to rely increasingly on knowledge-based rather than interest-based arguments to be heard (e.g. Seibicke 2020 on European Women's Lobby). When people from interest groups and industry participate on government-appointed advisory bodies – which is frequently the case both at the national level and in the EU – it is not only as representatives of specific interests but also as providers of knowledge. A recent example is the prominent role of experts from big pharmaceutical companies in the UK advisory body that dealt with the coronavirus pandemic, whose knowledge of the industry has been highlighted as a factor in the successful vaccine rollout.

Expertized politicians

So far we have discussed the various channels for providing expert knowledge to politicians and other policy-makers. But what about the expertise of politicians themselves? Recent studies suggest that the expertization trend extends even to politicians. In their book *Diploma Democracy*, Mark Bovens and Anchrit Wille argue that "most contemporary democracies are governed by a select group of well-educated citizens. They are diploma democracies – ruled by those with the highest formal qualifications" (Bovens and Wille 2017, 1). They show how the share of parliamentarians and ministers with higher academic degrees has increased sharply in several countries, far outpacing the share of the population with higher education. For instance, 90 percent of the members of the British House of Commons had a university degree in 2015, and the same share of Dutch MPs had a college or university degree in 2012. In comparison, only about a third of the electorate had higher education. In other words, although there are no formal qualifications required to hold political office, higher education has become a *de facto* prerequisite, excluding large swathes of the population.

Particularly in times of crises, there seems to be a hunger for "expert politicians". For instance, in Latin America during the 1990s and in Europe during the euro crisis, several countries appointed professional economists as finance ministers, prime ministers or presidents (Markoff and Montecinos 1993, Alexiadou and Gunaydin 2019). We saw the same tendency during the coronavirus crisis. In Italy, Mario Draghi, PhD economist and former head of the ECB, became prime minister of a national unity government at the height of the pandemic in 2021. His government also included Marta Cartabia, professor of constitutional law and former president of the Italian Constitutional Court, as Minister of Justice. In the Netherlands, Robbert Dijkgraaf, a theoretical physicist, string theorist and professor at Princeton and the University of Amsterdam, was appointed Minister of Education, Culture and Science in early 2022. The appointment of expert politicians may be driven by a genuine need for expertise to address difficult policy challenges. For instance, the Draghi government is widely seen to have mounted a successful coronavirus response. But placing an expert in high political office also has a symbolic function: it signals to the outside world that the government is competent and responsible, thereby strengthening its legitimacy with other states and international organizations and the trust of the financial markets (Markoff and Montecinos 1993).

There are of course cross-national differences within this general trend. In some countries, academic credentials are expected of top politicians. In Germany, for instance, PhDs are not uncommon among the political class. In Angela Merkel's third government, seven ministers had previously worked at a university and nine ministers had a PhD (Bovens and Wille 2017, 3). This is less so in some other advanced democracies. In Norway, for instance, master's degrees or PhDs have not been crucial qualifications for high political offices. Norway has had a long string of finance ministers without higher education beyond the bachelor's level and in most cases without any formal background in economics. Other countries again have frequently resorted to technocratic governments. Italy, for instance, has over the past 30 years alternated between regular political governments and technocratic cabinets composed of experts – and in some cases, political governments led by experts. Even though this tendency to depoliticize governing has drawn fierce criticism from populist parties, the 2018–2019 populist coalition government composed of the League (*Lega*) and the Five Star Movement (*Movimento 5 Stelle*) was headed by Giuseppe Conte, a professor of law.

In this chapter, we have put some empirical flesh on the notion that contemporary democratic governance relies heavily on experts and expert knowledge. We have provided a brief overview of the many channels through which expertise is incorporated into policy-making, ranging from the crucial role of ministry and agency bureaucracies as providers of expert knowledge and advice, via the proliferation of government-appointed expert advisory bodies, to the growing role of external suppliers of advice such as think tanks and consultancies. Even politicians are not immune to expertization, it turns out, as ministers and members of parliament are increasingly highly educated. But there are also significant variations within this broad expertization trend, as expert advice mechanisms and the involvement and influence of expert actors in policy-making differ across systems. With this multifaceted and variegated empirical picture of expert involvement in policy-making fresh in mind, we now turn to the normative discussion of expertise in democratic policy-making.

3 Expertise in democracy

According to Abraham Lincoln's famous dictum, democracy is "government of the people, by, and for the people" (1863/2009, 323). The first two parts of the dictum, "of" and "by", refer to the ideal of self-government: citizens are to be the authors of the laws and policies they are subject to. The third part of the dictum, "for", says that this kind of government will also result in laws and policies that are for the benefit of those governed. The assumption is that self-governing citizens will know what is good for themselves, and therefore make better laws and policies than a benevolent autocrat declaring that he wants the best for the people.

These two aspects of the democratic ideal – citizens shaping binding laws and policies, and the goodness or quality of their collective decisions – correspond to an often-made distinction between procedural and outcome-oriented standards of democratic legitimacy (Scharpf 1999). The procedural standard assesses legitimacy in terms of citizens' equal opportunities for participation in political decision-making, whereas the outcome-oriented standard evaluates the substantive quality of the outcomes of this process. Some theorists of democracy focus only on the procedural dimension and hold collective decisions to be legitimate if they result from decision procedures that give equal consideration to each citizen. What makes democracy valuable to them is this equality-respecting property, not its eventual potential for good outcomes or problem-solving capacities. However, they differ in their views about what the ideal of democratic self-government means, what it requires in terms of participation and how to make it feasible under conditions of political disagreement and social complexity.

Other theorists claim that procedural fairness is not enough. To be justified, democratic procedures must also have instrumental value. In Lincoln's words, what needs to be proved is that "government by

DOI: 10.4324/9781003106555-4

the people" also in some sense will be government "for the people". A purely instrumentalist view would be that democracy is valuable only to the extent that it contributes to some good outcome, identified independently of the democratic process, for example, political stability, economic efficiency, well-being or a more egalitarian distribution.

One group of theories, so-called epistemic theories of democracy, attribute instrumental value to democratic procedures because of their ability to generate decisions that have epistemic qualities such as being well-informed, well-founded and impartial. The assumption is that the likelihood of epistemically good or correct outcomes is greater with democratic procedures that include the many than with other less inclusive or more elitist procedures for making collective decisions. Epistemic theories are purely instrumental when they value democratic procedures only because of their epistemic properties. However, most epistemic theories also value democratic procedures for their intrinsic, egalitarian properties.[1]

Opposite the idea of epistemic democracy, there is a long tradition going back to Plato of epistemic criticisms of democracy arguing that the sovereign – "the people" – lacks the competence to shape good laws and policies. Alluding to Lincoln's dictum, Joseph Schumpeter stated in his critique of the "classical idea" of democracy as self-government: "If results that prove in the long run satisfactory to the people at large are made the test of government *for* the people, then government *by* the people ... would often fail to meet it" (Schumpeter 1942/1995, 256).

In this chapter, we will take a look at the controversies over the meaning and value of democracy and how they relate to our question about the proper role of expert knowledge in democracies. Broadly speaking, proceduralists tend to be skeptical toward "expertization", because extra political power to experts is inimical to political equality, while the attitude of instrumentalists depends on how "expertization" affects the quality of outcomes. We start with epistemic criticisms of democracy and arguments for epistocracy, a rule of knowers. We then turn to proceduralist and epistemic accounts of democracy and discuss the tension between participation and deliberation in the deliberative conception of democracy. Overall, we share with epistemic democrats a concern for the quality of decisions. Still, this strand of democratic thinking has so far not taken the "the fact of expertise" seriously. Consequently, it has also failed to address the accompanying question of how democracies, while taking political equality seriously, can take advantage of the cognitive division of labor in modern societies (Christiano 2012).

Epistemic criticism of democracy

As old as the idea of democracy is the criticism that the rule of the many will be a rule by the ignorant. In *The Republic*, Plato argued that good governance required that either philosophers become kings or kings make themselves philosophers. Without "a conjunction ... of political power and philosophic intelligence ... there can be no cessation of troubles ... for our states, nor, I fancy, for the human race either" (473). According to Plato, there is an idea of the common good to which philosophers have privileged access and which it is the state's task to realize. He distinguished the wisdom of the philosopher king from different subordinate branches of knowledge, such as rhetoric, military and juridical expertise (*The Statesman* 304–305). None of these qualify as "statesmanship" (305): "The point is that genuine kings do not actually *do* things themselves; they *govern* people whose domain is doing" (305d). Statesmanship "is the branch of knowledge which is responsible not only for all of them [the branches of knowledge mentioned], but for the laws and every other aspect of the state as well, and which creates the best possible fabric out of these materials" (305e). This means that the Platonic state is not an expertocracy as we would conceive of it: it is not ruled by persons who are particularly knowledgeable in well-defined domains, but by those who possess a master knowledge about the political good. Democracy will turn into misrule because citizens in general lack the governing insights that constitutes "statesmanship" as well as the subordinate expert knowledge, at the same time as they easily fall victim to one kind of expertise, namely that of the rhetorician. Plato illustrated his argument against democracy by a parable about a ship where the sailors quarrel with each other about who is the "true" captain without knowing what a true captain must know (*The Republic* 488d).

Today's epistemic critics of democracy do not appeal to a metaphysical insight about the good, but follow Plato in distrusting the political capacity of the demos. One type of epistemic criticism refers to the extensive research, especially in the United States, that has consistently shown the lack of knowledge about political issues among voters. In *Against Democracy*, Jason Brennan portrays citizens as not only badly informed, biased in their processing of political information, narrowminded and unable to relate to contrary points of view, but also as "rationally ignorant", that is, they choose to be ignorant given the cost of being informed compared to the chance of influencing the outcome with their vote (Brennan 2016; see also Caplan 2007, Somin 2013). If one thinks, as Brennan does, that democracy is "just a hammer", that is, primarily a tool or instrument to make decisions (Brennan, 11), and if most people are like he describes them, it can be tempting to recommend a distribution of political power "according to competence, skill, and the good faith to act on that skill" (Brennan, 14) to avoid incompetent rule and achieve outcomes that are "better, more efficient, and more substantively just" (Brennan, 53). Brennan's suggestion is that only citizens who pass a competence test should have the right to vote.

Against Brennan, it can be argued that democracy not only has instrumental value; that he exaggerates the negative evidence about citizens' competence; and that there is a democratic response to "ignorance", namely, to provide citizens with information and civic education instead of taking the shortcut of limiting participation to those who prove competent. However, the real puzzle is how it can be that Western democracies have performed quite well historically even though citizens certainly did not always live up to the ideal of being well-informed and public spirited (without thereby necessarily corresponding to Brennan's dismal picture). The short answer to this question is that democracies can perform quite well if they are bound by the rule of law, have an efficient and impartial administration, delegate specialized issues to expert bodies and have arenas for a reflective or deliberative formation of political opinion.

Still, no matter how competent the citizens and their representatives may be, there will always be epistemic asymmetries and dependencies – a fact of expertise – which will increase with the growing complexity of political issues and the amount of specialized knowledge required to deal with them. Democracies therefore tend to be cognitively overburdened. Based on such a diagnosis, the German political theorist Helmut Wilke has advocated expert arrangements that do not exclude incompetent citizens from taking part in elections – or give an extra vote to more educated citizens, as John Stuart Mill once suggested (Mill 1861) – but grant more power to different expert bodies to increase the overall steering capacity of the political system. Wilke refers to this as a "decentering of democracy" that further develops already existing forms of delegation of authority from the legislature to specialized, non-majoritarian institutions, such as constitutional courts and central banks (Wilke 2016). Philip Pettit (2004) has argued in the same direction within the framework of deliberative democracy. According to him, delegation to "de-politicizing" bodies is necessary in a deliberative democracy to prevent familiar epistemic deficiencies of citizens' deliberation (the role of passions, moralization and sectional interests) from having an impact on public decisions. Critics, on the other hand, worry that these "decentering" and "depoliticizing" responses in fact represent disfigurations of democratic rule itself (see Chapter 5).

Epistemic criticisms of democracy are based on two assumptions. First that there are some standards, independent of democratic procedures, according to which political decisions can be good or bad and, second, that there are some people who know these standards and how to apply them better than others (Estlund 2008). Democrats may take different positions on these two assumptions. Those who are normative skeptics or nihilists, of course, reject the first one, and embrace a pure proceduralist view, while those who think that questions about what is politically right can be subject to reasonable argument will accept it. Regarding the second assumption, democrats of the latter kind may accept that there is expertise in political matters, although they may have greater confidence in the political wisdom of the many, the demos.

But regardless of what epistemic competence a democrat believes the demos possesses, s/he will reject the "epistocratic" conclusion that the most knowledgeable should rule. S/he may do this because of distrust: also knowers can be corrupt; they can act out of self-interest; they may err; and their rule may turn into despotism. But the basic democratic objection is that political authority does not follow from epistemic authority. To be legitimate, a rule of the knowers must be generally acceptable, meaning that it must meet the consent of the less knowledgeable who must agree upon who the true knowers are (Estlund 2008). However, if epistocracy as a form of government cannot pass this general acceptability test, this does not preclude all kinds of delegation of power from a democratic legislature to separate expert bodies. Following Wilke's and Pettit's arguments, such arrangements – an epistocracy by democratic delegation, so to speak (Holst and Molander 2017) – may be a functional answer to the circumstances of politics in complex and scientized societies and to the deficiencies of public deliberation. The question is how these bodies can be held accountable (see Chapter 6).

Procedures only?

Pure proceduralism gives a straightforward answer to the epistemic criticism of democracy. Democracy is not about "truth", "knowledge" or "problem-solving" but about fairness. What makes democracy better than other forms of government is that decisions are made according to procedures that respect and include citizens as equals, not that it produces outcomes that are "good" according to some substantive criterion, for instance, welfare, freedom or distributive justice. As Nadia Urbinati puts it: "A bad decision is equally legitimate as a good one, when made according to democratic rules and procedures" (Urbinati 2014, 231). Pure procedural accounts of democracy take political disagreements to be so deep and pervasive that they cannot be settled by reasons, only by decisions that citizens can regard as rightfully made (Waldron 1999). Since majority rule is a procedure that is content neutral and treats all views equally, it could give legitimacy to collective decisions under conditions of disagreement. Climate realists and environmentalists, the radical secularist and the religious fundamentalist, or left-wing socialists and right-wing libertarians are unlikely to come to agreement on arguments and conclusions, but may all regard a majority decision as legitimate even if they happen to disagree with its content.

However, pure proceduralism has several problems. First, the idea that only procedures matter seems to contradict everyday political practice. Without the assumption that there are better or worse political decisions, why at all debate our disagreements instead of just observing them? If all that matters about decisions is that they are derived from the correct procedures, why are we still concerned with the substantive quality of outcomes and continue our disagreements after they have been correctly settled? (Lafont 2020) Take a decision about a new pension system, an environmental tax or a school reform; why defend or challenge it if a majority supports it, and why should the majority answer the minority? Second, the proceduralist presupposes a principle of equal concern and respect which in effect places restrictions on which outcomes are acceptable. For example, decisions that violate the freedoms presupposed in the democratic process, such as freedom of expression and the right to vote, will be illegitimate. Hence, taking its own standard seriously proceduralism cannot be purely procedural after all.

Third, and important for our purposes, proceduralists evade the fact of expertise. On the one hand, they fear that introducing a concern for decision quality, and so for the competence of decision-makers, may compromise political equality: "once *episteme* enters the domain of politics the possibility that political equality gets questioned is in the air because the criterion of competence is intrinsically inegalitarian" (Urbinati 2014, 83). Still, they do not confront the tension between competence and equality as a problem for democratic theory. It is a fact that some know more than others on certain issues, and we all profit from the epistemic division of labor in society; none of us is capable of or needs to be an expert on all things. If there is no way of making cognitive inequalities compatible with principles of democratic equality, then democracy does not seem like a viable form of government. To be sure, proceduralists may very well acknowledge that political decisions benefit from being based on the best available knowledge, but their theory of democratic legitimacy does not provide the means for dealing with the "fact of expertise". While dismissing "expertization" and "depoliticization", they also bypass the question of how expert knowledge can be integrated into and contribute to democratic decision-making. In addition, there is little they can object when legislative assemblies decide to delegate powers to expert bodies as long as the decisions are procedurally correct.

Turning Plato upside down: the epistemic dimensions of democracy

As an alternative to pure proceduralism, democratic theorists have recently tried to answer the epistemic critique of democracy directly by, so to speak, turning Plato upside down: rather than undermining democracy, epistemic considerations work in favor of it (Goodin and List 2001, Anderson 2006, Estlund 2008, Landemore 2012, Cerovac 2020; for overviews, see Peter 2008 and 2009 Rinderle 2015, Schwartzberg, 2015). According to these epistemic democrats, procedures of democratic decision-making do not only have the intrinsic quality of treating citizens as free and equal, but also the capacity to deliver better decisions then other procedures for collective decision-making. There are two main arguments for democracy's epistemic qualities. The first argument is aggregative and claims that majority vote itself has epistemic merit. The other focuses on deliberation, or the exchange of opinions and arguments that precede voting.

The classical and still much discussed aggregative argument is the French Enlightenment philosopher and mathematician Marquis de Condorcet's so-called jury theorem.[2] According to the generalized version of this theorem, the democratic aggregation of votes itself – one person, one vote – has epistemic properties. More specifically, in a question with two answers, one right and one wrong, the majority answer is probably the correct one (and the probability increases with the size of the group), provided that the individuals in the group have more than a 50 percent chance of being correct, and vote sincerely and independently of each other. Given these conditions, the theorem provides a proof for the truth-tracking ability of majority decisions.

A less formal argument for the advantages of group decision can be found in Aristotle's "doctrine of the wisdom of the multitude" (Waldron 1995). In *Politics*, Aristotle argued that "the many can, who are not as individuals excellent men, nevertheless when they have come together, be better than the few best people, not individually but collectively" (III, II, 1281a41) because they can pool their diverse knowledge, experience and insight. However, the pooling mechanism that Aristotle had in mind was not primarily an aggregative but a deliberative one. It is when people meet and talk with each other that this kind of wisdom occurs. To that extent, his argument differs from Condorcet's theorem, and not least from Rousseau's theory of the general will which was expressedly non-deliberative. Rousseau expected this will to emerge in its most appropriate or authentic shape "when citizens had no communication one with other" (Rousseau 1762/1973, 185) because communication involved the risk of demagoguery and factionalism.

The argument that public deliberation has epistemic merit is often traced to John Stuart Mill. In *Considerations on Representative Government,* he claimed that a body can deliberate better than individuals can do for themselves, and when it is "necessary or important to secure hearing and consideration to many conflicting opinions, a deliberative body is indispensable" (Mill 1861, 102). In a representative government, the "proper business" of the assembly is "talking and discussion"; the assembly is a "place where every interest and shade of opinion of the country can have its cause even passionately pleaded" (117). That the exchange of diverse opinions is conducive to the search for truth was Mill's famous defense of the freedom of expression in *On Liberty*. The silencing of an opinion was, according to him, in fact more harmful to those who dissent from it than to those who hold it because if the opinion is right, "they are the deprived of the opportunity of exchanging error for truth"; if it is wrong, "they lose, what is almost as great a benefit, the clearer perception and livelier impression of truth, produced by its collision with error" (Mill 1859/1989, 20). This truth-tracking feature of a free exchange of opinions is the basis for the expectation that a deliberative mode of decision-making will promote decision quality. Still, despite his vision of "government by discussion", to use Walter Bagehot's phrase (Bagehot 1872), and belief in deliberation's potential to eliminate the wrong opinions and strengthen the correct ones, it is disputed whether Mill was an epistemic democrat, and not just an epistemic liberal (Landemore 2012): he doubted the legislative competence of the representative body and limited its function to accepting, rejecting or remitting proposals from a Commission of Legislation consisting of legal experts (1861, Ch. 5), and defended a plural voting scheme, where the educated were given an extra vote, to prevent the ignorant from gaining as much influence as the knowledgeable (1861, Ch. VIII).

A more direct forerunner of the idea of deliberative democracy was the John Dewey. In *The Public and Its Problems* (1927), he tried to save the notion of a public which his contemporary Walter Lippman had dismissed as illusory – a "phantom" – in the age of mass democracy (Lippman 1925). According to Dewey, a genuine public will emerge through diverse and inclusive processes of public deliberation, where common interests are identified, and solutions to common problems are searched for. The crucial feature of democracy was not majority rule per se, but "antecedent debates, modifications of view to meet the opinions of minorities, the relative satisfaction given the latter by the fact that it has had a chance and that next time it may be successful in becoming a majority", and "the improvement of the methods of and conditions of debate, discussion and persuasion" was therefore an "essential need" (Dewey 1927, 208). A purely aggregative democracy would therefore be deficient. A group that votes on something must have decided to do so, and different options to decide on, and both require previous discussion: without initial public exchange, there can be no political agenda and no crystallized political alternatives.

This view of democracy was also formulated by one of Dewey's contemporaries, the legal theorist Hans Kelsen, who is not usually associated with deliberative democracy. In his *Allgemeine Rechtslehre*, he wrote:

> The will of the community, in a democracy, is always created through a running discussion between majority and minority, through free consideration of arguments for and against a certain regulation of a subject matter. The discussion takes place not only in Parliament, but also, and foremost, at political meetings, in newspapers, books and other vehicles of public opinion. A democracy without public opinion is a contradiction in terms.
>
> (Kelsen 1925/1945, 259f.)

When political will formation takes place in this way, and "the forceless force of the better argument", as Habermas later would call it, prevails, we have reason to expect that the political will also will hold a certain epistemic quality (being better informed, taking into account relevant views and interests, being less partial, etc.).[3]

Deliberative democracy and its discontents

In contemporary democratic theory, Condorcet's jury theorem has attracted a lot of interest. However, while no one disputes the mathematical proof, the assumptions about voters' opinions (that they are formed independently, that voters are more likely to be right than wrong, etc.) are demanding and have been modified and weakened by theorists who rely on the theorem (see, e.g. Grofman and Feld 1988). Moreover, political questions seldom have a simple binary structure. Public discussions about tax policies, how to organize hospitals or social services, or the approach to our neighboring countries or international organizations are often rich and will not be captured properly, but reduced, when summed up in a list of claims to which we then can say either "yes" or "no".

The idea that the core of democratic decision-making is not the aggregation of votes but public deliberation has been elaborated over the past 30 years in theories of deliberative democracy. This is a family of theories, with different origins, sharing the basic view that Kelsen articulated, namely that democratic rule is a "rule of reasons" (Forst 2001). Some deliberative accounts of democracy value deliberative practices primarily for intrinsic reasons – they express principles as mutual respect and a basic right to demand public justifications of laws and policies one is subjected to (see Gutmann and Thompson 1996, 2005, Forst 2001). Others emphasize (although not necessarily exclusively) that public deliberation will improve majority decisions by obtaining and disseminating necessary information, highlighting relevant aspects of political issues, clarifying which interests are affected and examining arguments for and against suggested problem solutions (see Nino 1996, Marti 2006, Peter 2009, Estlund and Landemore 2018). As Jürgen Habermas puts it: "embedding the will of the electorate and the formal procedures of decision-making in the vibrant and maximally unregulated circulation of public opinions exerts a rationalizing pressure towards improving the *quality* of decisions" (2009, 143; see also Habermas 1996, 304).

However, the extent to which decision-making processes in democracies in fact have argumentative qualities, how deliberation actually works and what it means for specific political outcomes are empirical questions, and a standard objection to deliberative democracy is that it is based on overly idealized assumptions (e.g. Mutz 2008a, Achen and Bartels 2016). Obviously, no deliberative theorist would deny the actual role of non-deliberative mechanisms in real-world political opinion and will formation. For example, Habermas (1996) regards interest-driven bargaining as completely legitimate. Also, and despite what is sometimes claimed by critics, the deliberative model is not based on strong assumptions about value consensus, but considers, in line with Rawls, disagreement about "the good" to be a fact of modern societies. Yet, it does assume that deliberation has the potential of transcending these disagreements by means of a more abstract agreement on "constitutional essentials" and principles of justice. Moreover, the model does not need to assume that all actors are committed to pursue common interests and the public good. Also strategic actors are typically forced to argue with reference to the public interest in a deliberative setting, because appeal to self-interest does not work well as a public argument. Public deliberation thus tends to promote impartiality. Jon Elster refers to this mechanism as "the civilizing force of hypocrisy" (Elster 1995), and we see it, for example, when interest groups try to adapt and frame their demands (e.g. a teacher union's demand for higher salaries or the oil industry's demand for lower taxes), not primarily as something that is in their own interest, but as something that is in everyone's interest (if teachers are better paid, schools will be better; lower taxes ensure higher productivity and job creation, etc.).

During recent years, there has been an empirical turn in the deliberative camp of democratic theory where scholars study whether deliberation works, and how (for overviews, see Mendelberg 2002, Thompson 2008, Karpowitz and Mendelberg 2018). The results of this research are mixed. It points in different directions, not least depending on the context of the deliberation, and on who the participants are. The most encouraging results arguably come from artificial settings, where representative population samples are given relevant and balanced information and the opportunity to contemplate and discuss over time in well-moderated discussions (e.g. Fishkin 2009; see also Dryzek et al. 2019 for an overview). Studies of parliamentary deliberation (Bächtiger et al. 2007) show that the chances for deliberative quality are highly dependent on institutional and issue factors and on actor characteristics. There are also no clear findings about the effects of deliberative quality on substantive outcomes, for example, whether decisions have an egalitarian, neutral or inegalitarian profile. Skeptics argue that citizen deliberation under ordinary conditions has a tendency to fail in rationality. People are not particularly willing to hear the other side, and democratic discourse systematically tends to produce opinions that disregard the best available evidence as defined by the relevant scientific disciplines (see, e.g. Sunstein 2002, 2006, Pincione and Tesón 2006, Mutz 2008b).

To overcome the objection that deliberative democracy is too demanding for mass democracies, Habermas as well as Jane Mansbridge and colleagues have proposed approaches to deliberation that do not focus on single forums, arenas or events (Chambers 2012). Here, public deliberation does not require face-to-face deliberation and active involvement of all citizens, or an ability to take part in all kinds of politically relevant deliberation. It is the system as a whole that is expected to ensure that public deliberation can improve political decision-making. In Jürgen Habermas' center-periphery model of political communication (1996, 2009), the media-based public sphere constitutes a mediating body between, on the one hand, deliberation and decision-making in and in close connection with formal political institutions and, on the other hand, the opinion and will formation that takes place in and through civil society's many associations, public events and movements as well as through informal conversations between citizens. The public sphere is seen as a "discovery context" where problems are identified, understandings of them articulated, and relevant information and different positions continuously formulated and debated before they are channelled into and filtered through the more regulated and problem-solving oriented parliamentary deliberation. The key factor in this model is the pressure that a vibrant public sphere can exert on the decision-making in parliamentary assemblies in the form of a continuous influx of problems, information and reasons.

Like Habermas, Mansbridge and her colleagues outline a "deliberative system" with more or less formal, more or less limited parts or arenas with different functions (Mansbridge et al. 2012). The parts of the system have their deliberative strengths and weaknesses and contribute differently to the overall system. Unlike Habermas,[4] they explicitly address the use of expert knowledge and ask how it relates to three functions that public deliberation is supposed to fulfill: the epistemic function of ensuring "reasonably sound decisions", the ethical function of promoting "mutual respect among citizens" and the democratic function of promoting "an inclusive process of collective choice". For example, deliberation in expert committees has an important epistemic function, even if their participatory credentials are weak and the delegation to experts is in tension with the norm of political equality. Other parts of the system may instead score higher on democratic parameters, for instance, on representativeness, but lower on epistemic criteria. But the function of improving the epistemic quality of decisions may also be in tension with the other functions of deliberation. A major ethical worry is that experts may behave in a patronizing way. Experts should set aside "ignorance, emotional volatility, and myopia of the non-expert", but this may also generate "disrespect for citizens' contributions and even for citizens themselves" (Mansbridge et al. 2012, 14). The fundamental democratic worry is that expertization may threaten democracy itself by excluding ordinary citizens from processes of deliberation. We will return to these worries in the next chapters, focusing on different kinds of epistemic worries in Chapter 4 and on democratic (and ethical) concerns in Chapter 5.

Deliberation and participation

As we have seen, much of the debate about deliberative democracy revolves around the relationship between its two dimensions, the democratic or participatory part, and the deliberative and allegedly rationalizing part (Elster 1998, Lafont 2006). Surely, not all deliberation is democratic (discussions can be exclusive and for the few), and discussions with broad participation do not necessarily have much deliberative quality (think of many social media debates). Still, it remains that without equal opportunities of participation, decisions are not democratic, and without deliberation, decisions are less likely to have epistemic quality.

Arguably, if the emphasis is on the epistemic dimension and on procedures that optimize deliberative quality, the expectation would be a trade-off between participation and deliberation. Consider, for instance, science or the court room. These are contexts where we are particularly concerned about the quality of the deliberation in order to guarantee the most correct outcome possible (be it valid scientific findings and theories or legally correct verdicts), and where discourse therefore is bound by argumentation requirements and participation is limited to those who are competent (see Holst and Molander 2009). Consider also the classic argument for political representation as a "filter" to ensure deliberative quality (Madison 1787/1987; see also Fishkin 2009), that is, where deliberation among trusted representatives is assumed to launder preferences and promote decisions that serve the public interest.

Likewise, there may be reasons to deliberate in closed forums issues that are in themselves public affairs (Chambers 2004). Publicity can in fact contribute to lower deliberative quality. In a comparison between the closed Constituent Assembly in Philadelphia in 1787 and the open one in France in 1789, Jon Elster found that the debates in the former were "remarkably free from cant and remarkably grounded in rational argument", while those in the latter "were heavily tainted with rhetoric, demagoguery, and overbidding" (Elster 2000). Another example is a study of the Federal Reserve which shows that when the discussions were made public, the willingness to express dissenting views diminished (Meade and Stasavage 2008). In line with this, and in a time where "transparency" in public affairs is increasingly on the agenda and often considered a requirement for good governance, policy advice committees often opt for closed proceedings on the assumption that it better ensures sound negotiations and deliberations than maximal public and media exposure.

The tension between deliberation and participation is intimately related to the unequal distribution of knowledge and deliberative capacity (Bohman 2000). Some know more about matters of relevance in a political process than others and may be better at reasoning about them. The widest possible participation can therefore come into conflict with deliberative quality. This is the standard objection from epistemic critics of deliberative democracy. Lack of knowledge about political questions and of rationality in the formation of political opinions makes it illusory to believe that inclusive publics will have the ability to bring out the best arguments in political matters (e.g. Brennan 2016). Democratic proceduralists, on the other hand, will fear that deliberative democracy may turn into epistocracy if the epistemic dimension of deliberation is emphasized at the expense of its participatory function, namely to make as many and different voices as possible heard and taken seriously.

Deliberative democrats' answer to both parties is usually that inclusiveness and rationality can somehow be combined, for instance, if there is an interconnected system of deliberative arenas and institutions linking civil society to decision-making bodies (cf. the deliberative systems approach or Habermas' (1996, 2009) communication model of deliberative politics). Rather than making deliberation less inclusive, the remedy of the problem of competence is to involve people in deliberation at different levels in order to make them more informed and able to form reasoned political opinions (Lafont 2020). Others try to link the epistemic properties of deliberation directly to democratic inclusion by appealing to theories about "collective intelligence" or "the wisdom of the multitude" (Landemore 2012 see below).

Yet, there is no quick fix. There *is* a tension between the two components of deliberative democracy (Fishkin 2009). It can be mitigated but not dissolved or eliminated. This becomes clear when we take into account "the fact of expertise". To be on par with the complexity of political issues, democratic decision-making must rely on contributions from expert communities. But to what extent can public deliberation relate to expert judgments relying on scientific theories and methods and still be inclusive? What if expert deliberations are better at finding solutions to collective problems or dealing with rights issues than more democratic forms of discourse and decision-making? For example, in a discussion of democracy at the supranational level, Habermas once argued that one has to reduce the expectations of participation compared to the national level and gave priority to public deliberation as a source of legitimacy:

> The democratic procedure no longer draws its legitimizing force only, indeed not even predominantly, from political participation

and the expression of political will, but rather from the general accessibility of a deliberative process whose structures grounds an expectation of rationally acceptable results.

(Habermas 2001, 110)

In later writings, he has abandoned this prioritization and is anxious to insist that deliberation and participation are inseparable and equally important sources of democratic legitimacy; without equal opportunities of participation all affected interests cannot be taken into consideration (2007, 433f; 2009, 146 f; 2013, 69; see also Dietelhoff 2009). This is certainly a basic democratic intuition, but a feasible theory of democracy has to face the potential trade-offs between deliberative rationality and participation, as Habermas did in his reflections on "the postnational condition". The requirement that all affected interests should be taken into account does not directly imply the widest possible inclusion. Interpreted not as a principle of organization but as a principle of *justification*, the requirement can be observed also in deliberative arrangements with low degree of participation.

Democracy or epistocracy?

The anxiety that a focus on the epistemic qualities of political decision-making may end up in epistocracy has been taken seriously by epistemic democrats such as David Estlund and Hélène Landemore. For them, it is imperative to show exactly why democracy is preferable to epistocracy.

Epistemic arguments for democracy can be more or less demanding. A minimal argument is that "democracy is at least as good as, and occasionally better than, a random decision procedure at making decisions, although it can be inferior to rule by the wise few or the lone genius". The maximal version of the epistemic argument for democracy is the idea that "democracy is at least as good as, and occasionally better than, any alternative decision rule" (Landemore 2012, 8). Estlund is an exponent of the minimal, and Landemore of the maximal version. Estlund does not assume that democratic rule will outperform an "epistocracy of the educated" (2008, 207). On the contrary, it is not unlikely that "removing the right issues from democratic control and turning them over to the right experts would lead to better political decisions, and more justice and prosperity" (Estlund 2008, 261–262). Nevertheless, he dismisses epistocracy. For political authority to be legitimate, it must meet the requirement of "qualified general acceptability", and since there are reasonable disagreements concerning who the right experts are, a rule of knowers cannot meet this requirement.

That we cannot know who the experts are is one of the classical objections against the expertization of politics (see Dahl 1989), and whether Estlund effectively blocks an epistocratic conclusion with this argument has been disputed (Lippert-Rasmussen 2012). One thing is that we do not completely lack criteria for deciding who is an expert and who is not (see also the chapters that follow). Another problem is that the argument seems to sit uneasily with Estlund's view on legitimacy (Brennan 2013): we often agree on principles without agreeing on how to interpret them more specifically, and if epistocracy can only be legitimate when there is no reasonable disagreement regarding the criteria of identifying experts, it is equally unclear how democratic decisions can satisfy the general acceptability requirement given the many reasonable views on how general political principles should be interpreted and implemented.

According to Landemore's maximal argument, democratic deliberation and decision-making have the capacity to epistemically outperform a group of knowers, even if we could identify in advance and agree on who the knowers are (Landemore 2012, 3). At the core of her argument, involving a set of different democratic procedures, aggregative as well as deliberative, is the Diversity Trumps Ability Theorem developed by Hong and Page. This theorem says that under certain conditions, cognitively diverse groups are better problem solvers than less diverse groups of individually more capable persons (Page 2007, ch. 6). Since larger groups are usually more diverse, Landemore generalizes this diversity theorem into a Numbers Trump Ability Theorem. However, even if the first theorem should hold,[5] it is not necessarily so that an epistemically optimal diversity is also the most inclusive: why not include only those who contribute with either their ability or their diversity (Marti 2013, Ancell 2017)? And, given what we know about voters' ignorance and about how political preferences are formed by group identities (Brennan 2013, Achen and Bartels 2016), how can we assume that "collective wisdom" will outperform expert judgments? The Hong-Page theorem may be less an argument for inclusive democratic procedures than for large and diverse bodies of knowers (Brennan 2016, 184).

Importantly, since Landemore and Estlund's primary concern is to explain why we should prefer a democratic regime to an epistocratic one, they tend to sidestep the question of the proper role of expert arrangements *within* a democratic order. Landemore makes a comparison between democracy and oligarchy when both are "equipped with a competent army of experts" and concludes that "democracy should still, on average and in long terms, outperform oligarchy" (Landemore 2012, 204). But she does not discuss the role of what she calls "the technocratic branch of government".[6] Arguably, this neglect of the executive part of the state and its expertise is something that Landemore shares with contemporary normative political theory more generally (see Heath 2020). Still, she seems to consider the delegation of authority to expert bodies unproblematic as long as it is made according to democratic procedures (Landemore 2012, 204). This approach makes it difficult to determine to what extent policy-making can be legitimately delegated to experts, as long as doing so is licensed by elected parliaments, and as long as one could reasonably expect this to result in better, more efficient and even more equitable decisions, than decisions made by a democratic assembly or directly by the plebiscite.

"Blind deference" and the fact of expertise

When we are concerned with the use of expert knowledge within democracy, a crucial question is what kind of deference to expert judgments it requires. In her sophisticated defense of a participatory conception of deliberative democracy, Cristina Lafont (2020) criticizes different "shortcuts" in contemporary democratic theory which bypass inclusive public deliberation and require citizens to "blindly defer" to others. "Blind deference" is, in her view, "quintessentially incompatible" with the idea of self-government. Although Lafont has little to say about the reliance on expertise as a circumstance of deliberative democracy, her "blind deference" test can be applied to expert arrangements and the question of how they can be made compatible with democratic requirements.

According to Lafont, epistemic justifications of deliberation miss the point with public deliberation. Although epistemic democrats are right in focusing on the importance of democratic deliberation for improving the quality of political outcomes, this cannot be the exclusive or even primary justification for deliberative democracy in the same way as it cannot be sufficiently justified on purely intrinsic ground. Lafont's worry about purely epistemic arguments is the familiar one; that they may lead down a slippery slope to epistocracy. According to her, what makes inclusive deliberation necessary is that it enables citizens to take part in the project of collective self-government: they can see themselves as "authors" of laws and policies which they are subject to and "obey them based upon insights into their reasonableness" or "reflectively endorse them" (18). Public deliberation is about convincing co-citizens, reaching reasoned judgments and developing a considered public opinion. Without democratic deliberation, citizens cannot "equally own and identify with the institutions, laws, and policies to which they are subject" (3).

Lafont's yardstick for evaluating political institutions and practices in light of the ideal of self-government is whether they require of "blind deference" to the judgments and decisions of others. Theories of democracy which take "shortcuts" around democratic participation and attempt to remove political decisions from public deliberation to avoid problems of modern democracies, such as overcoming disagreements, political ignorance and low quality of public deliberation, will not pass the blind deference test. Representative democracy demands deference to others, but not *blind* deference, as long as there are mechanisms that ensure equal and effective opportunities for citizens to shape the political process and prevent alienating misalignments between the policies they are subject to and their interests and ideas. This means that democracy can be participatory "but not in the sense of requiring citizens to be involved in all decisions" (23).

The situation is different, according to Lafont, with, for example, "deep pluralist" views on democracy which use majority rule as a shortcut for solving the problem of political disagreement. This shortcut preserves the norm of political equality but gives minorities no other choice than "blind deference" to majority decisions. Other types of shortcuts that Lafont identifies are the "epistocratic" and the "lottocratic" ones: the first recommends blind deference to expert judgments, the latter to decisions of a randomly selected group of citizens (a mini-public). In the following, we will discuss what her rejection of "blind deference" implies for our approach to expert bodies, given "the fact of expertise".

Generally, if we take "blind deference" to mean deference without any reason, this is probably not what we see in cases where citizens and their representatives rely on expert judgments and legislatures delegate the treatment of various issues to expert bodies. To be sure, recognition of expertise by individuals and institutions is more or less trust-based, and in many cases, this trust may seem close to "faith" (as Giddens contends, see Chapter 1). Yet, trust in experts is not necessarily and seldom completely blind. That is, even in situations of deep epistemic asymmetry where lay people are not able to review and assess expert reasoning, there are criteria and clues for judging trustworthiness and for what is an acceptable use of arguments based on trust in epistemic authority (Walton 1997, Goldman 2001; we will discuss some such criteria in Chapter 4). Hence, if non-blind deference is defined as deference with *some reason*, quite extensive reliance on expert judgments and delegation to expert bodies may be acceptable. Even with a stricter concept of non-blind deference, requiring well-considered judgments about the trustworthiness of putative experts, it is unclear which uses of expertise in political decision-making that we know from contemporary democracies would prove to be unwarranted. Entrusting tasks to experts entails, as all principal-agent relationships, agency risks (experts may misuse their expertise and make mistakes), and hence there is a need for accompanying mechanisms to ensure experts' performance (see Chapter 6).

However, it could be argued that Lafont's concern is not deference based on considerations of epistemic trustworthiness at all. From her perspective of democratic self-government, what is of interest is "blind deference" in a specific political sense: citizens defer blindly to the decisions of some agent if they cannot rule out a misalignment between their interests, values and considered judgments and the agents' decisions (9, 24). In such a situation, citizens are not able to identify with laws and policies that they are subject to and to endorse them as their own. To avoid such political alienation, citizens must have effective and equal opportunities to exercise control over political decisions. Accordingly, under this interpretation of "blind deference", the space for expert arrangements in democracies will be smaller than under the pure epistemic interpretation of "blind deference". We may have good epistemic reasons for trusting the judgments of a group of non-elected experts, but lack reasons to assume that their political agenda will coincide with ours.

However, even so it is unclear what kind of expert arrangements the "blind deference" test rules out. Does delegation of decisional power to expert bodies as such place citizens in a state of alienation where they cannot take a position on whether the decisions are based on reasons that they could reasonably endorse? Take the delegation of monetary policy to a central bank as an example. If political and economic arguments for an independent central bank are plausible, and the objectives of monetary policy are topics of public deliberation and decided by a democratic legislature which also reviews and controls how the bank fulfills its mandate; is this delegation compatible with the ideals of self-government as formulated by Lafont, or not?

Lafont indicates an answer in a discussion of Thomas Christiano's model for an interplay between deliberation among citizens and experts. Christiano argues that democracies should take advantage of the cognitive division of labor in modern societies to increase the "truth sensitivity" of politics (2012). He also makes the traditional distinction between means and ends, where experts can answer questions of means but not of ends. As long as citizens are in the "driver's seat" and choose "the basic aims the society is to pursue" (2012, 33), they can defer questions about means to credible experts. Along with many others, Lafont finds this distinction between means and ends too simple (see Chapter 1). According to her, legislation cannot be seen as just a means to achieve certain aims endorsed by a democratic majority that can be delegated to the deliberation of experts. The crafting of laws concerns the "fundamental rights and freedoms of citizens" and therefore requires citizen deliberation and mutual justification. This seems plausible (whether it hits Christiano is a different question). However, the insistence on the integrity of law does not answer the entire question about to what extent reliance on expert judgments is compatible with the ideal of a participatory deliberative democracy. Within the constraints of "fundamental rights and freedoms", policy-making involves complicated questions about probable effects and side effects of policies, and about how the choice of one end affects other ends, where expert judgments are likely to be needed. Moreover, there may also be need for "moral experts" – in the sense we have outlined in Chapter 1 – that can enlighten public deliberation about "basic aims", the costs of choosing certain means and how rights and freedoms constrain political decisions.

Later, in a reply to critics (2020), Lafont has also admitted that expert knowledge has a proper political role to play, as long as constitutional concerns are seriously taken into account,[7] and she seems to accept Christiano's model after all: "Experts can offer technical advice but have no particular right to impose their values and preferences upon their fellow citizens" (157). She illustrates this with the political debates concerning the global pandemic:

> Doctors, epidemiologists, economists, and other relevant experts can inform us of the difficult choices we are likely to face in light of a scarcity of medical resources or the potential collapse of different sectors of the economy, but they cannot make these choices for us. The citizenry as a whole must make the tough choices of deciding which economic risks are worth taking in order to save lives, which fundamental rights and freedoms are worth limiting in order to keep the economy going, how much personal risks first responders can be asked to take on, what the proper social compensation is for taking on that risk, and so on. The input of experts is necessary for answering these questions but it is obviously not sufficient. Citizens must take *their own risks* in light of *their own values and preferences*.
>
> (Lafont 2020, 157)

Yet, this statement of the proper use of expertise again leaves several questions open. For one thing, Lafont herself points to what we have called the fact of expertise as a "vexing question":

> If lay citizens lack the competence required to understand and process the highly technical knowledge involved in complex political issues, then how can experts properly 'inform' citizens so that they can make sound political decisions? The problem is compounded when the experts themselves disagree on the proper information and advice. How can lay citizens adjudicate among conflicting bodies of expert knowledge and advice if they themselves lack expertise in the areas in question?
>
> (Lafont 2020, 157)

Furthermore, it is not only the issue of "fundamental rights and freedoms" which makes it problematic to talk about purely technical expert judgments. Experts advising citizens and government often touch upon myriad normative questions, pertaining, for example, to the evaluation of levels of risks and distributive considerations. The intricate relationships between technical and normative issues raise important questions concerning the most proper organization of expert advice and delegation to expert bodies.

We will return to these questions in Chapter 6, in the spirit of the deliberative systems approach, and ask with Thomas Christiano: how can "a democratic society ... adequately utilize the intellectual resources a division of labour provides in a way that is compatible with the idea of rational discussion among citizens about policy and law" (2012, 29)? We will however first identify and assess different worries about expertise, epistemic as well as democratic, to enable a more specific and constructive discussion of the proper role of expert arrangements in democracy (Chapters 4 and 5).

Notes

1 On the divide between procedural and outcome-oriented approaches in democratic theory, see, for example, Peter (2008, 2009), Kelly (2012), Rinderle (2015), Fleuss (2021), Christiano (2022).
2 *Essai sur l'application de l'analyse à la probabilité des décisions rendues à la pluralité des voix* (1785).
3 See Habermas (1972/1984) for one early use of this expression.

4 Despite his early interest in the relationship between science and public deliberation (see Chapter 1), the role of expert knowledge is not explicitly addressed in his later model of political communication.
5 Brennan (2016, 181) has brought to our attention a critique of the mathematical foundations of the theorem by Abigail Thompson (2014).
6 This point is also made by Moore (2017, 25) and Moore (2014).
7 She answers Lisa Herzog's (Herzog 2020) question about the proper role experts in democracy.

4   Epistemic worries about expertise

Criticism of "expert rule" and an exaggerated reliance on expert knowledge is frequently heard in contemporary politics. Even during the coronavirus crisis, despite increasing trust in expert knowledge and scientists in record time providing us with an effective Covid-19 vaccine, experts and expertise came under fire. Many critics had democratic concerns and worried about the rise of a technocratic corona state where the rule of the people was replaced by a rule of pandemic professionals. But critics also worried about other things, for instance, about whether all the self-proclaimed corona experts were qualified and impartial, about experts' mistakes and misjudgments about the virus and how to contain it, and about how the dominance of medical and public health experts could overshadow the insights and perspectives of other expert communities or experiential and local knowledge.

This chapter focuses on worries of the latter kind, which we will refer to as *epistemic worries* about expertise (whereas the *democratic* worries are left for Chapter 5). Generally, what such worries have in common is a concern for policy and decision quality. The promise of including experts in policy-making is that policies will be more rational and informed and outcomes will improve. Experts are supposed to be the "filter" that ensures truth-sensitive policies and legislation (Christiano 2012). Epistemic critics of expertise, however, worry that relying on the advice of experts, at least if too much or in the wrong way, can be detrimental to the quality of governance and policies.

Strikingly, epistemic worries are often underplayed, if at all considered, by those who defend an increasing role for experts in policy-making (e.g. Pincione and Tesón 2006, Caplan 2007, Brennan 2016, Sunstein 2018), and evidence-based policy-making (e.g. Davies et al. 2000). Scholars in this camp typically fear "irrationality", "deliberative failures" and disregard for "evidence" when political decision-making is left to "the demos", but pay less attention to disagreements, biases

DOI: 10.4324/9781003106555-5

and mistakes among experts. At the same time, the epistemic critique of expertise coming from the opposite camp tends to be embedded in a rather sweeping discourse about "arrogant", "narrow-minded" and "interest-ridden" experts that is simplistic and does not distinguish between the range of different concerns that are involved. By unpacking the epistemic worries about expertization, this chapter seeks to address in more systematic terms the full range of the epistemic critique, and to prepare properly for our later discussion of how to better ensure that experts perform according to their promise.

Puzzlingly, epistemic critics have often had little concern for mitigating different forms of expert bias in policy-making. They have inferred pessimistically from the potentially adverse consequences of expertization for governance and policy-making that we either have to debunk expertise – and somehow make rational public policies without it – or live with its negative effects on policy and decision quality, hoping that the epistemic benefits of our expertise reliance will weigh up for the costs. We instead take a constructive approach and argue that these adverse consequences can be addressed by means of proper institutional design of expert bodies, but also of the larger political system in which expert bodies are embedded (this is the topic of Chapter 6).[1]

In what follows, we will first list ten epistemic worries about the political role of experts – worries that are all, as we see it, worthy of being taken seriously. We unpack the different worries drawing on different research traditions and on examples from current expert arrangements and recent public controversies. We then discuss what this list of worries does and does not imply and argue that even if the worries mentioned are potentially serious, there are also good reasons to rely on experts. Yet, we need to think systematically about how to ensure that experts act in accordance with our expectations to proper experts and make a positive contribution to the quality of contemporary governance.

1 Who are the "real" experts?

A first and fundamental epistemic worry is how to identify the actual experts. Who should pass as an expert in some domain? This is hard to know for sure. We often see how people disagree about who the "real" or "best" experts are. It is easy to say that decisions would improve if they were informed or even made by experts, but it is notoriously difficult to identify beyond controversy who are first-rate experts and who are second-rate, quasi-experts or simply non-experts in different cases. This is the "novice/expert problem" (Goldman 2001/2011).

As we have noted already (Chapter 1), laypersons in their assessments of which experts to put epistemic trust in will often need to consult other experts. However, how more precisely could consulting other experts be of help? For one thing, there may be competing claims to expertise – what Alvin Goldman refers to as the "novice/2-experts problem". When legal experts disagree on whether a national regulation is compatible with EU law, or when medical experts disagree on the evidentiary basis for this or that priority in health services, who should you side with? Goldman (2011, 116) lists some possible clues the novice might rely on when deciding who to trust, such as the argumentative performance of experts, agreement from fellow experts in the field, experts' track records, and evidence of interests and biases.

If one expert clearly performs better than others in an argumentative exchange, this may indicate that her conclusion is the more correct one. However, the ability of non-experts to assess experts' argumentative achievements varies. Sometimes it may be possible for most people to evaluate the consistency, accuracy and reasonableness of expert statements without extensive expertise in the field. In other cases, the problem is exactly that a real assessment of the quality of expert argumentation requires expert knowledge that non-experts lack. Consider, for example, debates on monetary policy. The European Central Bank says about its recently published papers[2] that they provide "the conceptual and empirical basis for policy-making" and are meant to "stimulate discussion", but also adds that "[the papers] are addressed to experts, so readers should be knowledgeable in economics" (European Central Bank 2022). In other words, non-experts will have a hard time evaluating the quality and soundness of the arguments and conclusions of the research that underpins ECB policy. Similarly, were economists to disagree on some of the conclusions that are made, the non-expert cannot easily form an informed and independent opinion on which of them to support.

Clearly, drawing a conclusion about expertise based on agreement from fellow experts may be sound, but is not unproblematic. To what extent does the fact that more experts reach overlapping conclusions indicate that these conclusions are correct? There are many examples of how putative experts have got it wrong (Hirschi 2018, Koppl 2018). Consider, for example, how many psychiatrists supported lobotomy as a treatment for mental disorders, or the many cases of known miscarriages of justice caused by investigators, lawyers, expert witnesses and judges' misinterpretation of evidence. According to Goldman, experts' independence from one another is crucial: there are reasons for laypeople to consider the relative number of experts that approve of a statement or a theory if the experts in question have reached their conclusions independently of one another. But if experts support other experts without any independent investigation or extra thought, then expert consensus is actually of little value, and non-experts may just as well rely on their own judgments. If so, we are once more confronted with the general layperson/expert problem.

This is also the case if laypeople are to choose among competing experts based on their track records, because to do so, they must in the end be able to assess these experts' achievements. Both during the corona crisis, and recently, when foreign policy experts analyze the war in Ukraine, scholars with seemingly excellent credentials disagree both in their explanatory analyses and in their recommendations about what to do. It is then up to non-experts to somehow decide who are the "better" experts and who to rely on.

Non-experts also have the option of ranking experts on the basis of possibly distorting influences from interests (we return to this later in the chapter). For instance, they might be wary of medical experts who are paid by big pharmaceutical companies, or social scientists who are also active in a political party. Yet, even if interests should be part of laypeople's assessments, they cannot be decisive. On the one hand, an expert statement can be correct even if the expert in question has an interest in it being correct. To take the most obvious example: if a genuine expert argues that we should take her advice, it will often also be in her interest that we take it; being listened to may increase her agenda-setting power, social status and personal satisfaction, get her more job offers, etc. However, this does not imply that her advice is incorrect. On the other hand, there are disinterested experts who may possess little expertise on the case at hand (consider a natural scientist with an impeccable record within theoretical chemistry who advises on action to address climate change), or if they do have substantial insight in the case at hand, they may still make mistakes or have biases (consider the climate scientist who relies on flawed models).

Moreover, evidence on pecuniary interests is more accessible for a novice than the subtler influence of biases. We may be able to detect a medical expert's personal economic interests in government approval of a certain treatment, at least if proper transparency and control mechanisms are in place. It is harder to trace normative or disciplinary biases that may draw the expert more toward some conclusions than others. If all or most members of a community of experts have the same bias, it may be even harder for an outsider to detect it.

Finally, going beyond Goldman, laypersons may have others to consult as well regarding which experts to trust. Experienced and well-informed politicians, policy-makers, newspaper editors and columnists, and leaders of civil society organizations and interest groups may have both considerable knowledge in relevant domains and advanced skills in communicating with broader audiences, and often point at some experts as more trustworthy than others. Such guidance may be more or less well-founded, but generally stands on more shaky ground than often admitted. Either such intermediary figures qualify themselves as experts – they may, for instance, pass as "interactional experts" of the kind we discussed in Chapter 1. Yet, if so the above listed problems apply: even if interactional experts are good communicators, epistemic asymmetries will make it hard for non-experts to check their explanations directly. If politicians, journalists and others who guide citizens regarding which experts to trust, do not qualify as experts, they are themselves not in an epistemic position to check on experts' analyses and judgment directly. How then can we trust them? Finally, intermediary figures and interactional experts among policy-makers, in civil society and the public sphere, often have interests and biases of their own, and on this basis cherry-pick or unintentionally lean toward experts of their liking.

Clearly, when we add up all of this, there is plenty to be genuinely worried about. On paper, it seems like a good idea to consult expertise, but if we in the end cannot identify with much certainty who the genuine experts are, it is reasonable to question whether our reliance on those who present themselves as experts is really good for policy and decision quality.

2 There are no moral experts

As we have noted, expert advice typically involves not only technical considerations, but also normative judgment. We often see appointed experts enter what Kant referred to as "the Kingdom of Ends" and take on an ethical role. This can be initiated by the experts themselves, for instance, when climate scientists or researchers on poverty and human development add ethical considerations or passages that emphasize the moral urgency of immediate action to their scientific analyses and scenarios. However, experts may also be mandated and asked by governments to make normative considerations. For a very explicit example, consider the recent Norwegian Gender+ Equality Commission. This commission, consisting exclusively of researchers and university professors, was asked in its mandate not only to report on "the current status, and possible improvement", of Norway's gender equality policy "in the intersections between gender, ethnicity, and class", but also to develop a "principle-based" defence of why gender equality and gender equality policies are "important to pursue". Obviously, to answer this brief, the expert group needs to cross the boundary between facts and values.

In other cases, descriptive and prescriptive considerations in expert analyses and recommendations may be hard to disentangle. Consider, for instance, two recent Norwegian expert reports on taxation.[3] The two reports discuss factors that affect capital flows and access, and the effects of different tax policies on a range of macro-parameters. However, the interplay of empirical and normative considerations in such reports tends to be intricate, and in the end, it is difficult to establish exactly on what grounds the two commissions recommend significantly different tax schemes, even if it goes without saying that two reports that recommend opposing policies in a politically contested area cannot be considered as purely technical.

Obviously, this does not mean that it is not possible to come a long way in distinguishing technical advice from normative assessment after proper analyses, even in such murky cases. Arguably, the more fundamental problem is that experts selected on the basis of their credentials in providing factual analyses and technical considerations do not necessarily have much extra competence in handling moral issues. We have already argued that some people are likely to be better at inquiring into normative questions than others and better equipped to argue in a convincing and informed way for priorities and ways of dealing with conflicting norms and values, and so, that there can be "moral expertise", in this sense (see Chapter 1). However, typical governmental experts – lawyers, economists, engineers, etc. – may have little in their education or experiences that prepare them for such tasks. Expert advisory reports that are solid in their analysis of causes and empirical consequences are often extremely meager when it comes to explication and discussion of goals and normative principles. This was also evident during the coronavirus crisis, when medical experts on viruses and epidemics in many countries slipped into advisory roles that involved making moral judgments on whether it was a good thing to close schools or keep the economy open – leading to accusations that the experts were posing as politicians. The explanation and justification of these judgments were often lacking, stated very implicitly, extremely superficial or questionable.

Moreover, in policy-making contexts, normative considerations may be no less complex than technical considerations. For instance, returning to Norwegian expert commissions, several of them deal not only with issues that are technically complicated and esoteric, but also initiate ethical deliberations on advanced levels that may be difficult to grasp for non-experts. One example is a commission on insanity defense in criminal law that includes a detailed philosophical and conceptual analysis of notions such as "autonomy" and "responsibility" (NOU 2014a). Another example is a commission on priority-setting in health care that addresses complex redistributive questions based on theories of justice (NOU 2014b). Hence, epistemic asymmetries can occur in discussions of ought-issues (just as they occur in discussions of is-issues) and make it hard for non-experts to directly assess the soundness and validity of arguments (Bertram 1997). This task becomes even harder when seemingly credible experts disagree in their treatment of normative questions, such as questions of distributive justice or on how to deal with conflicts between rights or between collective goals and individual rights. Who should you then trust?

3 Use of expertise requires scientific consensus and social stability

For the novice to separate "real" or "the best" experts, be they technical or moral, from less trustworthy advisors also becomes harder in times of scientific shifts and societal crises. Generally, scientific fields or disciplines are characterized by competing paradigms or research programs and, after periods of production of expert knowledge within the parameters of a certain cognitive framework, tend to undergo shifts that change the notions of what qualifies as expert knowledge. The sources of such shifts can be internal to the expert community, spurred by theoretical or conceptual innovation, methodological breakthroughs or new technologies. Examples from the economics discipline are the marginalist revolution around 1870, the Keynesian revolution in the 1930s and the break up from the postwar consensus on the synthesis of neo-classical micro- and Keynesian macroeconomics in the 1970s and 1980s, which all fundamentally changed the tenets of the discipline about how the economy works and how it should be studied. More recently, the rise of behavioral economics has challenged basic microeconomic assumptions about the rational behavior of actors. Another recent example is the use of powerful data processing programs and big data in the social sciences, which has strengthened one side in the long-standing controversy between those who think that hypothesis-testing and quantitative analyses are the only basis for true knowledge and those who believe that more inductive approaches and qualitative data can offer valuable insights.

Shifts in expert knowledge and intensified competition and dis-agreement between expert communities can also be related to social and cultural changes, economic crisis or political ruptures. One well-known example of externally spurred changes is how the rise of new countercultures and social movements during the 1960s changed knowledge interests in the human and social sciences, as a new generation of scholars developed novel research programs to study gender, racism, and domestic and global inequalities. The Keynesian revolution took place against the backdrop of the Great Depression, and the turn away from Keynesian economics to monetarism and supply-side economics was partly a response to the economic crises of the 1970s. More recently, the 2008 financial crisis spawned renewed interest in Keynesian economics (see, e.g. Akerlof and Schiller 2009) and widely different interpretations within the economics community of what caused the crisis and what remedies were needed. Some attributed the crisis to an economic and financial system built on neoliberal orthodoxy, others to flawed political choices made without due regard for economic models. Economic experts also differed in their policy recommendations, with some favoring an austerity approach and "market conforming" measures, whereas others criticized austerity and emphasized the need for more "market shaping" measures (Jabko 2010, Blyth 2013). In such situations of crisis and upheaval, when expert knowledge is contested and in flux, identifying the "true" expertise become even harder for the non-experts.

4 Experts make cognitive errors

To the extent that proper experts can be identified, it is generally reasonable to assume that they, when they use well-established scientific methods and follow the rules of scientific reasoning, are less prone to make errors than laypeople. Nevertheless, experts make mistakes, and when they do, there is little reason to believe that their advice will lead to better policy. Research in cognitive psychology has shown that expert judgments are more exposed to fallacies than we like to think and that statistical models in many cases outperform case-based expert judgments, which are subject to various cognitive biases (Mehl 1954, Tversky and Kahneman 1974, Tetlock 2005, Mercier 2011, Kahneman 2012). The general problem is that humans – including experts – have a limited capacity for information processing and therefore tend to make inferences on the basis of heuristics or shortcuts which can lead them astray and cause biases.[4]

Experts have a dubious reputation as forecasters as well, because of their overconfidence and confirmation bias. In *Expert Political Judgment,* Philip Tetlock (2005) presents results from studies of experts' ability to make economic and political predictions. Their answers to questions scored bad on accuracy, especially if they were "hedgehogs" who "know one big thing" in contrast to "foxes" who know "many things". The average expert did about as well as those who do random guessing, or "dart-throwing chimps". Tetlock himself has regretted this harsh judgment and criticized the way his research has been used to dismiss the qualifications and key role of experts as such (Tetlock and Gardner 2016; see also Quirk 2010). Moreover, in a follow-up project, Tetlock and his colleagues asked thousands of people to make predictions about world events. Some of them proved to be extraordinarily accurate, and when they worked in teams, they performed even better. What made them good at predicting was their "foxlike" problem-solving strategies, how they gathered information, how they reasoned and how they related to new information (Tetlock and Gardner 2015). Interestingly, these "super-forecasters" were not necessarily experts on the issues in question, and the key to their success was their avoidance of the cognitive strategies that characterize overconfident experts.

Accusations of bad forecasting among experts are recurrent in real-life policy-making as well. Economic forecasts for the EU economic area and the Eurozone have, for example, been criticized for being based upon uncertain, unlikely or even random estimates, resulting in poorly founded scenarios and recommendations, and, in the end, failed policies. A standard accusation is how the Commission and the ECB made their estimates during the early 2000s clearly having "no clue" about the upcoming crisis and recession.[5] Later, they failed to foresee the recovery. However, the problem coming to the fore in this criticism is not so much that expert predictions are conceived as decisively false or flawed, but that experts operate too confidently and exaggerate the certainty of estimates that are key to their problem framing and recommendations.

Expert judgments of events in the past might be equally biased. A common error in expert investigations into major crises and disasters is hindsight bias, namely, the tendency to judge behavior in the past based on information that we have now. Failing to take into account what actors knew at the time may lead experts to draw erroneous conclusions about the actions taken in response to crisis. This may in turn lead to wrong "lessons learned" (Renå and Christensen 2020). For instance, the expert report that examined the 2011 terrorist attacks in

Norway partly assessed the emergency response based on information that was only retrospectively available and based on the effects of the actions taken rather than on whether the actions were warranted at the time (Renå 2017).

5 Experts are one-eyed

There is an old saying that if the only tool you have is a hammer, everything looks like a nail. Experts are no doubt often too confident in their own competence (Angner 2006), they identify with their disciplines and are prone to frame problems so that they fall within their disciplinary matrices, paradigms or "epistemic cultures" (Buchanan 2004, Lamont 2009). Different expert disciplines look at the world through distinct theoretical lenses. These lenses are what allows experts to analyze a problem: they bring some aspects of the issue clearly into focus. For example, engineers, lawyers and economists will tend to approach environmental policy differently: engineers will typically focus on technology, lawyers on regulation and economists on taxes and dues (Tellmann 2012).

The downside is of course that other aspects of the issue are defocused and thus ignored. Consider once more the Black Lives Matter mass demonstrations that took place during the coronavirus crisis and how they exposed the blind spots of disciplinary expertise. For epidemiologists, these demonstrations were potential "super-spreader events" that needed to be avoided at all costs. From an epidemiological point of view, a mass demonstration is no different from a large group of people standing closely together at a football game or a music festival. In other words, medical experts were "blind" to the different character of these gatherings; their theoretical lenses directed the attention directly and solely at the problem of virus transmission. By contrast, many political scientists, looking through their own theoretical lenses, saw the demonstrations as an essential element of democracy that could not be subordinated to public health measures. (Of course, these political scientists were often equally blind to the epidemiological consequences of the demonstrations as medical experts were to the democratic ones.)

These kinds of disciplinary perspectives can color the analysis and recommendations of expert advisory bodies. The expert commission investigating the 2011 terrorist attacks in Norway (NOU 2012) concluded, devastatingly, that the attacks could and should have been prevented, and recommended "that leaders at all levels of the government administration work systematically to strengthen their own and their organization's fundamental attitudes and culture" regarding "the acknowledgement of risk", "implementation capacity" and "result-oriented leadership". However, this conclusion was not clearly supported by the evidence. Instead, the recommendation appeared to reflect the domination of lawyers and people with business sector background and management expertise on the commission, which resulted in a narrow focus on legal regulations and obligations and on attitudes and culture instead of on structure and organization (Renå and Christensen 2020).

Thus, when expert advice does not cover all relevant aspects of and perspectives on an issue, but rather reflects specific disciplinary viewpoints, citizens are right to worry about the quality of advice and poorer quality of policy and outcomes.

6 Experts have self-interests

Another not unreasonable worry is that experts may be more or less biased by their self-interests and may use their epistemic monopoly to their own advantage (Koppl 2018).[6] A statement from the philosopher Robert Spaemann in a 2008 German parliament commission on the permissibility of using human embryonic stem cells in research may exemplify:

> I take the liberty of a final remark on the status of the "experts" questioned. As an independent authority can only be considered whoever is not committed to a particular interest by his professional status. Thus, not researchers working with embryonic stem cells or representatives of research institutions under whose ceiling such research takes place. They are an interested party and must be viewed as competent lobbyists. Their ... advice must be relativized and deserves no more hearing than that of a reflective nurse.
>
> (cited in Zenker 2011, 362)

To be sure, in a well-functioning political system, manifest conflicts of interest are normally taken care of by the procedures for the selection of experts. However, interests may be hard to detect, for instance, when medical researchers have long-term interests in findings of successful treatment, because of increased funding opportunities.

Moreover, even if there are no direct ties to parties who are interested in a certain outcome, experts may favor research findings that are to their own advantage. A well-known problem is the bias toward findings that are statistically significant (Nuzzo 2014). Articles with statistically significant results are easier to publish in academic journals than articles with null findings. This means that researchers who care about their academic prestige and career have an interest in finding statistically significant effects. This may lead to questionable research practices such as running analyses until one "finds something" (also known as "p-hacking"). It also implies that published findings provide a distorted picture of the actual effect of a variable, since null findings are rarely reported and just-significant findings are over-reported (Simonsohn et al. 2014). All of this may bias the expert knowledge decision-makers rely on to formulate policies.

Similarly, experts may have a self-interest in findings that confirm positions they have defended, be it in academic or more public settings, and so bolster their professional reputation. This has been an issue in the context of Norwegian expert commissions. For instance, in the case of the recent Drug Reform Commission, critics worry that the experts in the field will be unable or unwilling to give arguments for legalization a fair chance since they have invested their careers and prestige in the current criminalization regime.

7 Experts are ideologically biased

In addition comes the charge that experts have ideological commitments or other deeper normative orientations that influence their judgments. In some cases, experts may have an explicit ideological or political outlook that colors their advice. This concerns, for instance, knowledge providers such as think tanks that have a specific ideological commitment, say, to libertarian values or social democracy. Think tanks of this kind may have staff with expert credentials and may present themselves as independent providers of knowledge to policy-makers. Yet, there is an obvious tension between their commitment to certain values or political causes and their ability to provide objective and impartial expert advice (Christensen and Holst 2020).

More generally, experts of all kinds will have moral orientations and political views, whether they themselves explicate them or not, and these may affect their research and advice. For instance, academics are more left-leaning than the general population on most political issues (Gross 2013). In a recent study from Norway, the Labour Party was the most popular party among social scientists, and more than 50 percent voted for either the Green Party, or parties to the left of the Labour Party. Critics on the political right see this as a source of ideologically biased advice and as a reason for doubting the credibility of certain types of social science experts, such as sociologists. Critics may also be concerned about the political views of experts on specific issues. For instance, in the case of the expert commission on Norway's agreements with the EU, opponents of Norwegian EU membership worried that experts who are in favor of membership would be unfit to give a balanced assessment of Norway's EU relationships due to strongly held pro-EU views.

One can object that the political views of academics do not necessarily affect their research and knowledge-based advice, in part because research is subject to academic norms of impartiality and procedures such as peer review. Yet, political values may still have subtle effects by influencing a researcher's choice of research topic or theoretical perspective, especially within the social sciences (Rolin 2020).

Finally, numerous examiners of social science from Gunnar Myrdal (1930/1953) onward have noted how theoretical approaches of academic disciplines may frame the problem at hand in such a way that some value options are tacitly favored. For example, neoclassical economics frames problems in a way that tends to favor efficiency in the allocation of resources over distributive effects. This is one reason why expert commissions dominated by economists are often accused of promoting market-conforming measures and "neo-liberalism" in different areas of public policy and administration. Importantly, the charge is not, or at least not primarily, that the economists in question are politically conservative; in the Nordic region, many economists rather lean toward social democracy and support labor governments. According to critics, the problem is rather that dominant approaches within economics have a systematic and inherent pro-market bias. Sociologists, by contrast, who are concerned with "solidarity" (in the Durkhemian sense), "social integration" and "class" tend to be critical of markets and "commodification" and are often attributed with an anti-market and communitarian mentality.

8 Experts will not speak truth to power

A concern may also be that experts belong to and identify with the societal or "power elite", and that their elite position and frame of reference compromise their independence. Experts are supposed to "speak truth to power" (Wildavsky 1979). Yet, their connections to the "establishment" tend to make them more affirmative than critical of the powers that be. This suspicion is a common ingredient in populist politics and its distrust of experts (Caramani 2017). But it is also fuelled by sober sociological and political scholarship on elite recruitment, formation and networks (Rahman Khan 2012). Academics and other experts tend to have similar social backgrounds as political and business leaders.

Most obviously, these groups all tend to have higher education, which sets them apart from the majority of the population (Bovens and Wille 2017). Experts also often interact with other elites, for instance, in policy-making networks. Fulfilment of the duty of truth-telling (what the Greeks called *parrhesia*) requires courage because it may involve personal risks (Foucault 2001). When experts have so much to lose in terms of resources and connections, there is the worry that they will not risk compromising their elite peers for the sake of the truth.

A discussion along these lines has concerned the growing role of scientific knowledge in the Norwegian advisory system. Critics see an increasing elite bias in this scientization, for example, when the Gender+ Equality Commission lacked representation from women's organizations and civil society, or when a recent commission reviewing the role and tasks of school teachers included professors and researchers but no school teachers. Behind this criticism lies a democratic concern (see Chapter 5), but also a worry that elite commissions will reproduce convenient elite conceptions and prejudices instead of speaking up and speaking "the truth" in the interest of ordinary people.

Another variant of this worry is that experts will not speak truth to power because they, in different ways, are controlled by the political regime. Involving experts in policy-making will not contribute to better policies, since experts are simply "useful idiots" serving powerful political interests. The most expansive version of this critique – prominent in science and technology studies – has it that the very knowledge offered by expert disciplines is fundamentally shaped by the political context (e.g. Jasanoff 2004). Expert knowledge is part of and serves dominant societal discourses: economic science may serve to legitimate a neoliberal governance regime and business interests, medical experts may further a medicalized approach to health and boost the profits of big pharmaceutical companies, etc.

A narrower version centers on the political use of knowledge. Politicians often use expertise symbolically: by setting up expert bodies or appointing scientists to prominent positions, they seek to give the impression that policy-making is rational and knowledge-based; they are less interested in the actual advice offered by these experts (Weiss 1979, Feldman and March 1981). Decision-makers also use expert knowledge selectively: in a sea of expert knowledge, they will pick the advice that fits their predefined preferences (Boswell 2008). If that is the case, expert advice has little influence on the direction of policy and the result will be poorer policies (Parkhurst 2017). Policy-makers may also orchestrate or design expert advisory bodies in ways that make experts fall into line, as Annabelle Littoz-Monnet argues in her study of EU bioethics experts (Littoz-Monnet 2020). For instance, politicians and bureaucrats often consciously seek to steer the work of expert groups both through ex ante mechanisms such as the design of the terms of reference and the selection of members and through ex post mechanisms such as intervening in the discussions of the group (Hesstvedt and Christensen 2021).

9 Experts are bad at communicating their knowledge

The objection that experts lack the ability to communicate their knowledge resonates with common experiences. No doubt, experts are often bad at stating arguments in a comprehensible way: "People have a hard time taking the perspective of a less knowledgeable individual, and the gap is only wider for experts addressing laymen" (Mercier 2011, 321). For instance, experts have a tendency to write in scientific jargon and emphasize precision over simplicity. Because of elitist attitudes, experts may also be unwilling to communicate in ways that reach out more broadly to stakeholders and citizens. Experts may be more interested in sharing their latest research with the scientific community than in trying to spell out its implications for stakeholders who do not appreciate the nuances or precise scope of the findings. Incentives for researchers also play a role: in many systems, academics gain research funds and promotion by publishing academic articles in English-language journals rather than by writing op-eds in their national language or by talking to citizens and interested parties.

Such translation problems, whether due to experts' limited abilities, motivation or incentives, add to the already troublesome situation of epistemic asymmetry between experts and non-experts. Due to cognitive inequalities, it is hard for non-experts to grasp and assess the soundness and quality of experts' advice. If experts are also bad communicators, then the situation will only worsen.

10 Experts have poor political judgment

A last worry is that experts tend to lack "political literacy" (Eriksen 2020), that is an understanding of political processes and the ability to make political judgments, since many of them are prone to view political questions as if they were questions of facts and logic. On the one hand, this may result in recommendations that are "right", in the sense that they are supported by solid evidence, but that lack political feasibility, at least here and now. A version of this is when experts give unfeasible recommendations because they ignore institutional political conditions for their implementation (Swift and White 2008). Experts may propose reforms that lack political support, such as economic experts' insistence on more stringent taxation of owner-occupied housing. They may also recommend policies that do not fit easily with existing policies, such as proposals for universal basic income that come into conflict with extant welfare systems. This kind of mismatch between expert supply and policy-maker demand for policy advice may limit the ability to formulate effective policies.

On the other hand, experts may exaggerate the extent to which the space for political action is constrained by *Sachzwang*, by given circumstances and parameters. For instance, in the first phase of the coronavirus pandemic, British health experts advised the government not to impose a lockdown, in part based on the idea that people would not accept strict health measures. In this case, the risk is that experts to a too great extent embrace the assumptions of politicians and administrators about what is desirable and what is possible, rather than critically questioning these assumptions.

We have argued that all these epistemic worries and concerns are reasonable and potentially serious. They cannot be reduced to "populism", "knowledge resistance" and "post factual politics", and it is misleading and irresponsible when they are neglected by proponents of evidence-based policy-making and defenders of more political power to experts and expert bodies.

It must also be noted that whereas objections 4–10 are about expert failures and inappropriate use of expertise, objections 1–3 are of an epistemological nature and apply even under ideal conditions: if there is something like flawless expertise, objections 1–3 will still remain since epistemic asymmetry represents an inherent problem in all use of expertise, since descriptive and prescriptive issues tend to be intertwined in policy-making, and since over time there will be scientific and social shifts that change the basis for expert judgment.

Yet, these worries, however persuasive, are not reasons to debunk expertise. Despite expert disagreement and the difficulties non-experts have distinguishing real expertise from quasi-expertise due to epistemic asymmetries, genuine experts can in many cases be identified. And when expert institutions are organized and work well, non-experts can reasonably trust them. Experts make cognitive mistakes, but often they also perform well, and their shortcomings must not be exaggerated. It is true that experts may have disciplinary and ideological biases, private and social interests, or be prone to wishful thinking. However, this does not imply that they cannot give sober, qualified advice, and the fact that there are cases of bad expert performance should not make us blind to the myriad cases where experts genuinely contribute to more enlightened policy discussions and policies. Neither should we underestimate the engagement in many expert communities to communicate research to have impact and as a professional service to citizens and society.

Potential sources of bias are moreover often double-edged. That experts are committed to their discipline may make them narrow-minded, but disciplinary commitment is also a mechanism ensuring that they act according to shared epistemic standards and norms (Tellmann 2016). That experts have moral and political priorities may bias their investigations in unfortunate ways, but these priorities may be reasonable and shared by many non-experts and spur them to examine important societal problems with scholarly rigour.

In short, there are epistemic worries, but there are also a range of reasons to have epistemic hopes. Moreover, and fundamentally, despite the risks involved in putting trust in expertise, rolling back expertise is simply not a viable option due to the fact of our expertise reliance and the cognitive division of labor in modern societies. Experts can get it wrong and give poor advice, but in the end, we depend on them to make effective and just policies and sound and well-informed decisions. Our focus therefore should rather be on how to design and institutionalize expert advice and expert bodies to ensure that the epistemic worries become less worrisome and to increase the likelihood of proper expert behavior and performance. From this perspective, the worries we have discussed should not be perceived simply as sources of pessimism and despair, but also as incentives to make expert institutions better and expert communities more well-functioning. If there are reasons to worry that experts are overconfident, one-eyed, etc., we should try as far as possible to develop and cultivate expert communities and institutions that make these worries less urgent and relevant (see Chapter 6). But before we get that far, we need to discuss the democratic worries about expert reliance in policy-making. Whereas this chapter has surveyed different worries about whether experts actually contribute to better policies, the next chapter turns to the various worries about the adverse effects of expert power on democracy as rule by the people.

Notes

1 Hence, we do not see our approach as "pessimistic" (Mikalsen 2022). See also Rothstein (1998) on the constructive approach. Rothstein discusses how to make use of the often dismal findings from research on the implementation of public policies.

2 With titles such as "Monetary Policy, macroprudential policy and financial stability", "Liquidation value and loan pricing" and "Caution: do not cross! Capital buffers and lending in Covid-19 times".

3 NOU 2014c Capital Taxation in an International Economy (NOU 2014:13) and NOU 2018 Capital in Times of Conversion – Business' Access to Capital (NOU 2018:5).

4 As an example of how experts may make simple cognitive errors, consider, for instance, the experiment by David Eddy (1982). One hundred physicians were presented with the following case:

> A physician has encountered a slight lump in a woman's breast. He thinks there is a 1 percent probability that the patient has breast cancer. If the woman *does* have breast cancer, then there is a 80 per cent probability that mammography will detect this (she tests positive). If she *does not* have cancer, there is still a 10 per cent probability that she tests positive. What is the probability that a woman who tests positive has breast cancer?

Ninety-five physicians answered that the probability was between 70 and 80 percent, whereas the correct answer is 7.5 percent. It seems that the physicians made use of the so-called representativeness heuristics (Tversky and Kahneman 1974, Kahneman 2012) and replaced the difficult probability question with a simpler one: How typical or representative is it that women who have breast cancer test positive? (Eddy 1982, Kirkebøen 2009)

5 See, for example, www.opendemocracy.net/en/european-economic-forecasts-why-do-they-get-it-wrong/

6 Koppl (2018) argues that experts use their expertise, their human capital, to provide expert opinion as a commodity to be paid for. Experts choose what information to provide, and an epistemic monopoly is likely to result in poor expert performance.

5 Democratic worries about expertise

Whereas epistemic worries regarding experts' political role have received limited attention by defenders and critics of expert rule, democratic concerns have been much more pronounced. We know the unvarnished version of the democratic critique of elites and experts from the populist discourse of for instance former US President Trump and the Brexiteers in the United Kingdom. According to populist ideology, which "considers society to be ultimately separated into two homogeneous and antagonistic groups, 'the pure people' versus 'the corrupt elite'" (Mudde 2004; see also Müller 2016), experts belong firmly in the second category. Experts are usually seen as part of the establishment and thus as opponents of the people and the idea that politics should be an expression of the popular will (Caramani 2017). Populist politicians have therefore challenged scientific knowledge about climate change, vaccines and economic policy and pushed to "take back control" from unelected experts in national bureaucracies and international organizations.

However, democratic criticisms and worries over the political role of experts are prevalent in many quarters and go far beyond populist attacks. Consider, for instance, the recent critique of the shortcutting of democratic procedures and the rise of a public health technocracy during the coronavirus crisis, or the more long-standing debate on the democratic deficits of the EU. Consider also the critique of the power of economists over economic policy, and of the influence of lawyers in bureaucracies and courts over a broad range of regulative issues, which are at odds, it is claimed, with ideas of political equality and our democratic self-conception. Finally, consider controversies, for instance, on climate policy or gender equality policy. Some claim that more power to climate scientists or gender experts will contribute to make the world a better place. Others worry about the rise of a quasi-authoritarian "do good" environmentalism that disregards democratic concerns and

DOI: 10.4324/9781003106555-6

about the expansion of a feminist technocracy, be it national state feminist machineries or the "femocracies" in organizations such as the UN and the EU, that set the agenda on "gender" with little input from civil society and ordinary citizens.

Even those who enthusiastically embrace a larger role for experts and "evidence" in governance tend to recognize and grant that there are democratic problems with simply delegating a broad range of political decisions to experts. However, these problems are in the end brushed aside, and considered "solved" in systems where there are free and fair elections and where the final decisions are made by elected politicians.

By contrast, we believe there are a range of democratic worries about experts' political role worthy of closer consideration, even in relatively well-functioning democracies. Just as we in Chapter 4 listed several distinct epistemic worries, we will in what follows unpack the different democratic worries raised by critics of expertization. As with the epistemic worries, the democratic ones are not seldom misleadingly conceptualized and exaggerated. Even if there are genuine democratic problems with relying too much or in the wrong way on expertise in governance, there are also ways to incorporate experts and expert knowledge in policy-making in full-fledged democracies. In other words, the worries we list in this chapter should not spur us to roll back expertization altogether but rather to design our expert bodies and political systems more wisely (see Chapter 6).

1 Expert power is at odds with democratic self-government

The most basic democratic objection to experts' political role is that it is inimical to the idea of "rule by the people". Democratic procedures give each and every citizen an equal say in shaping collective decisions they are subject to. As we saw in Chapter 3, some democratic theorists focus on this intrinsic value in their justification of democracy (see, e.g. Christiano 2008). We believe in democracy not primarily because of its problem-solving capacities but because it is the best institutional expression of our understanding and recognition of each other as free and equal citizens. Due to the fairness of procedures, democratic decisions can claim legitimacy in the sense that they can be acceptable also for those who disagree with the decisions. To those we referred to as pure proceduralists, the instrumental credentials of democracy are even irrelevant. Whether delegating agenda-setting or decisions to scientific experts provides us with better policies, say on welfare, taxes or education, is beside the point. Granting the knowledgeable extra political power endangers democracy regardless of whether it produces better outcomes.

But which procedures are fair in the sense that they properly express the idea of political equality? Many would point to free and fair elections of legislators and decision-making based on majority vote as decisive. This notion of democracy as election-based majority rule is also central in contemporary democracy research. A branch of this research develops international democracy indexes that seek to measure comparative levels of democracy around the globe. These indexes are compound measures based on a range of indicators where free and fair elections are consistently conceived of as fundamental.

Still, majority decisions do not end disagreements, only settle them temporarily, and in a democracy, minorities can go on to challenge these decisions; they do not have to "blindly defer" to the majority (see Chapter 3). Accordingly, also procedures that limit the will of the majority and demand qualified justifications of laws and policies are expressive of the idea of political equality. Non-majoritarian expert bodies that collect and produce knowledge of factual basis and policy effect may be crucial for citizens to assess such justifications. Interestingly, studies of citizens' conceptions of democracy show that rule of law and governments offering justifications of their decisions are central also to citizens' *de facto* conceptions of democracy, in addition to free and fair elections (e.g. Kriesi 2018).

That expertization of political decision-making is in tension with "rule of the people" is obvious. But there are also tensions between democracy and bureaucracy and between democracy and the rule of law, and just as well-functioning and just democracies depend on both bureaucracy and the rule of law, democracies satisfying epistemic desiderata are dependent on making use of expertise. This means that democracies face the challenge of how to integrate expertise in governance in ways that are compatible with democratic deliberation and electoral democracy. Hence, the worry about democratic self-rule should definitely be taken seriously, yet primarily as a warning against giving so much power to experts that democratic legitimacy is undermined (see worry 3 below).

2 Wisdom rests with the many, not with the few knowledgeable

The opposite camp in democratic theory, the epistemic democrats, turns the objection from proceduralists upside down (as discussed in Chapter 3). Their contention is exactly that democracy's legitimacy as a form of rule depends on the truth-tracking qualities of its procedures.

As we have seen, this argument is seen by some as a slippery slope toward epistocracy. However, epistemic democrats argue that democracy actually tends to deliver comparatively well from an epistemic point of view or even better than an imagined epistocracy. The problem with expertization then is that it may lead to poorer outcomes, since there is an alleged "wisdom of the many" that makes them collectively wiser than the most knowledgeable (Landemore 2012). To be sure, this objection is about potential epistemic loss, but it still belongs among the democratic worries, since it is based on the assumption of a "democratic reason" (to quote the title of Landemore's book on the topic) that may be set aside or constrained by expertization.

Are the many wiser than the few? To what extent is there "reason" in democracy? Notions of experts as arrogant, disconnected from reality, ignorant regarding issues outside their narrow field, lacking political judgment, etc. are common, and scholars within science and technology studies and from the perspective of deliberative and participatory democracy argue that we need to include the perspectives, knowledge and judgments of ordinary, non-expert citizens. They have brought forward a range of cases and controversies where the inclusion of local and stakeholder knowledge and the views, risk perceptions, and priorities of citizens and civil society representatives arguably has improved the decision process, for instance, in disputes over resources and environmental policy, and in cases of regulation of new technologies (Wynne 1992, Fischer 2009, Jasanoff 2012). Such inclusion may thus have the potential of ensuring "the simultaneous demand for epistemic and political authority" (Krick 2015, see also Brown 2009).

Recently, scholars have also tried to measure more systematically the wisdom of crowds compared to the wisdom of experts. It has been argued that the quality of, for instance, local government and budgeting (see, for instance, Legard and Goldfrank 2021 on "deliberative participatory budgeting"), climate policy, and constitutions (see Landemore 2020 on the French Citizens' Convention on Climate and the constitutional revision on Iceland) is improved by different participatory and crowdsourcing measures, and that such measures are superior to expert arrangements.

3 Expertization gives too much power to the unelected

However, beyond these fundamental democratic concerns, coming from the non-epistemic (1) or epistemic (2) camp of democratic theory, there are also a range of democratic worries concerning the legitimate scope for expertise in democracies. The need for expert advice and some delegation to expert bodies is generally recognized in many quarters. Yet, the fear is that expertization goes too far; that is, that there is a shift from elected to unelected power (Mair 2013). This concern has been raised regarding the European Union, since a wide range of decisions that were previously made by elected national governments are now shaped by unelected officials in the European Commission, the EU agencies and the European Court of Justice.

However, it arguably applies much more generally to the considerable delegation of powers to semi-independent agencies in many polities. For instance, in several countries, public health agencies were given the power to adopt wide-ranging measures during the coronavirus pandemic, including closing schools and businesses. The worry in such cases is partly that parliaments consciously and explicitly go too far in delegating political decisions, so that parliaments in effect illegitimately curtail their own democratically mandated power. But the concern is also that substantial decision-making power is *de facto* delegated to agencies in the shadow of parliamentarian acts of delegation with seemingly limited range, without parliamentarians' awareness, and so without a proper democratic mandate. A typical case is when a parliament gives a public health or other agency the task of providing technical advice; yet, the agency ends up making judgments regarding redistribution of goods and risks that extends well beyond the technical considerations MPs originally had in mind and foresaw. The unelected power of central banks to decide the level of interest rates – decisions with major effects on the economy and people's welfare – has become broadly accepted across the developed world. The argument has been that it is in everyone's long-term interest to shield the setting of interest rates from the electoral cycle and the short-sightedness of public debate. Hence, by delegating monetary decisions, parliaments bind themselves to the mast. Still, critics wonder why decisions with large economic and distributive consequences are not rather made by the majority in parliament, or rather why the majority decided to relinquish control of monetary policy.

4 Expertization harms public deliberation

Deliberative democrats (see Chapter 3) who stress the importance of public deliberation, there is additionally the worry that deliberation over political issues becomes dominated by experts, and so significantly *less public*. If too much emphasis is put on expert knowledge, this may unduly narrow the space of viable reasons and devalue the contributions of ordinary citizens. Once more, this worry may be compatible with recognizing the value of bringing expert knowledge into public deliberation and the need to defer to expert authority in many questions, and the hope is for a balanced interplay of expert knowledge and opinion formation in the public sphere (Christiano 2012). However, critics from the deliberative branch of democratic theory worry that the domination of experts causes a serious imbalance that harms public discussion and obstructs the proper functioning of the public sphere (Fischer 2009, Chambers 2017, Steiner 2017).

The difficulty of broad public deliberation around coronavirus measures may serve as example: as medical experts claimed to know best how to contain the virus and political leaders by and large called for "listening to the experts", there was effectively little room for deliberation about the measures involving a broader range of voices. Critical voices were easily dismissed as cranks or conspiracy theorists. The broad expertization of political life that we described in Chapter 2 has compounded this worry. Several countries and international organizations have seen an increase in the participation of academics and the use of scientific knowledge in policy advice. The leadership and secretariats of civil society organizations and interest groups in many countries are also largely dominated by people with master and PhD degrees, professional consultancy and think tanks are on the rise, and intellectuals, professors, private and public sector leaders and other people with higher education dominate among newspaper columnists (Bovens and Wille 2017). Overall, critics argue, these trends leave us with a public sphere that is narrower, less diverse and less deliberative; experts' claims and reasons take center stage and are scrutinized primarily by other experts, and not from a variety of angles and positions.

5 Expertization undermines bargaining among social interests

A range of other democratic concerns are also not necessarily *anti* expert, but take up problematic effects if expertization goes too far or takes the wrong track. Apart from voting and deliberation, bargaining is a central mechanism of political decision-making (Elster 1998). For those who emphasize the importance of bargaining in democratic political processes, there is the additional worry that the political role of experts interferes with a fair negotiation of social interests. The problem is in part that some interest groups in society are more capable of utilizing experts' cognitive resources than others, and that expertization will tend to come with increased and potentially undue influence for these groups (e.g. Albareda 2020). For instance, well-funded business groups have a greater ability than small-budget civil society organizations to establish think tanks and commission expert reports that can produce knowledge to influence policy-making. In addition, experts or particular expert communities will constitute powerful interest groups of their own. For instance, doctors may champion knowledge-based arguments to advocate for more funding for hospitals and medical research, whereas advocates for greater spending on youth social services may not have the same intellectual authority to back up their demands.

More fundamentally, the familiar grammar of politics comes under pressure: expertization facilitates talk about political outcomes and policies as more or less "knowledge based", "rational", etc., and not as reflecting some groups' values and interests. Whereas civil society organizations previously could justify their role as bearers of vital societal interests and concerns, they must increasingly argue that they also contribute with valuable competence, expertise and counter-expertise. Simply being an "interest group" or mobilizing for certain principles and priorities is seemingly no longer enough. Similarly, within economic and labor market policy, mechanisms for neo-corporatist bargaining are under pressure in many countries, whereas expert arrangements are increasingly influential.

We see this increasing emphasis on knowledge and expertise also in elected assemblies: the European Parliament has recently expanded its in-house research capacities to provide parliamentarians with more evidence-based input for policy-making. Hence, also in parliaments, it is seemingly no longer enough that representatives of the people simply reflect and promote certain preferences and interests (Bovens and Wille 2017). The expectation is increasingly that parliamentarians' proposal must be responsibly "knowledge-based". Some welcome this development, pointing, for instance, to the benefits of "more competent" and better informed politicians. Yet critics find this trend worrisome, because it may serve some preferences and interests better than others, such as those of parliamentarians with higher education, or interest groups with huge secretariats of knowledge workers. For instance, since policy preferences are closely associated with level of education, this development biases the political agenda against the concerns of the lower educated, such as fighting crime or limiting immigration (Bovens and Wille 2017, 146–148).

Also, interest promotion may become harder to detect and challenge when it is disguised as "superior knowledge", "the best available expertise", "evidence", etc. Discussions about what the evidence shows may obscure the social values at stake and privilege particular interests and aspects of a problem, for instance, those aspects that can be measured (Parkhurst 2017). This critique is frequently raised in cases where contested reforms or cuts in public spending to the disadvantage of some groups are justified not in terms of political priorities but with reference to experts' recommendations. A good example is the world-wide wave of tax reforms from the 1980s onward, which, for a large part, were inspired by microeconomic theory about the effects of taxation on the allocation of resources (Christensen 2017). Advocates of these reforms pointed to economic evidence showing the pathologies of existing tax systems and the benefits of lower tax rates and broad tax bases for economic efficiency. Critics saw this as little more than a smokescreen for a radical neoliberal policy shift that would benefit high earners and big business and increase the tax burden for regular people.

6 Expertization leads to political alienation

An additional worry is that expertization may increase the feeling among large shares of the citizenry that they live under a rule that rather expresses the will of experts and elites. This is what concerned Robert Dahl (1985), who argued that too much power to experts can produce "political alienation" among ordinary citizens (see also Chapter 3). Citizens will not be able to see themselves as authors of, and thus responsible for, the laws and policies they are required to obey. To put it with Thomas Christiano: many will not feel at home in the world they live; they will experience it as "a world where one does not see how legitimately to make it responsive to one's interests" (Christiano 2008, 62). Such feelings of alienation may produce disaffection and distrust among the large swathes of citizens who do not belong to the elite of experts and higher educated. Bovens and Wille show how in contemporary expert-dominated democracies, people with lower and middle education are much more likely than the highly educated to report that "government does not care what people like me think" and that they have "no influence on what government does", and they are much less likely to have trust in parliaments, politicians and parties (Bovens and Wille 2017, 155–158).

This political alienation and disaffection figures as a main explanation for many of the ills of contemporary democracies, including low voter turnout, populism and violent anti-system sentiment. The feeling that policies reflect the concerns and interests of the expert elite rather than what regular people want has been seen as contributing to the spectacular rise of populist movements across most Western democracies over the past decades (Mounk 2018). The election and near-reelection of Donald Trump as US President illustrated just how widespread this feeling of being left behind is, and in Trump's telling, experts are one of the main groups to blame. Similarly, disaffection with expert-led coronavirus policies sparked sometimes-violent protests across Europe against the restrictive measures, vaccines and the expert class behind these policies.

Some commentators see variants of populism as a response to the political alienation caused by the dominance of the knowledge elite that can boost political participation and the chance to be heard for those left behind (Bovens and Wille 2017, 166–167, see also Mansbridge and Macedo 2019 on "left populism"). Yet, clearly, there are expressions of populism that constitute nothing less than a fundamental threat to democracy, as when populist leaders challenge the very foundations of the democratic constitutional state. Glaring illustrations are the democratic backsliding in Hungary or Poland and the angry mob that stormed the US Capitol in 2021 to prevent the confirmation of the election results.

7 Experts lack respect for ordinary citizens

Furthermore, experts may tend to regard ordinary people as ill informed, and to define "good policies" as those that are based on "knowledge" and "evidence", irrespective of public opinion. These kinds of attitudes are sometimes labeled "technocratic" and involve not only a belief in science and expertise but also an elitist view that regular citizens are ill equipped to make decisions and a dislike of partisan and interest-based politics (Bertsou and Caramani 2022).

It has been argued that these kinds of attitudes are particularly common among certain expert communities with considerable political power, such as economists (Christensen and Mandelkern 2022), but also among the legal and medical professions. These are all professions where considerable influence on policies and regulations has gone hand in hand with technocratic preferences, but also with a deeper engagement for "technocratic utopias" and rational social planning undistorted by the ignorance of the man in the street (Steffek 2021).

Critics accuse experts with elitist attitudes of underestimating the cognitive abilities, information levels and common sense of ordinary people. Others concede that political ignorance may be widespread, but still worry about overconfident and condescending experts. To be sure, such experts may easily overlook their own biases and cognitive limitations and come to deliver analyses and recommendations of poorer quality. This is a recurrent accusation against economists, for instance, when very few of them managed to foresee or prepare governments for the 2008 financial crisis. Currently, similar charges are made against "the realist school" in international relations and political science, which is accused of arrogantly sticking to theoretical assumptions about strategic interests that make Russia's invasion of Ukraine "impossible" and almost incomprehensible. Also, during the coronavirus crisis, experts' arrogance was frequently mentioned as a cause of flawed policies.

Yet, importantly, these accusations are not only epistemic (of the kind we listed in Chapter 4). When experts are arrogant and condescending, they also place themselves outside the democratic community and its norm of mutual respect (Mansbridge et al. 2012): they fail to live up to epistemic standards, but also disregard the ethical requirement that members of a democracy, expert or non-expert, should treat each other respectfully and as citizens with equal standing.

8 Experts don't have "skin in the game"

Experts qua experts are moreover – or at least they see themselves as – "*freischwebende*" (free-floating), to use Karl Mannheim's (1936) term: their primary loyalties are often to epistemic communities or to their professions, and they tend to overlook the political context and the power relations in which their expert activities are embedded. This makes experts less capable of understanding the *modus operandi* of democratic politics and the motives of their fellow citizens: most people who engage in politics have particular attachments and identities and seek communities of like-minded. For instance, when citizens engage in political parties or in campaigns, their primary motivation is not to "hear the other side" or to find the best solution for all involved parties, but to engage in a genuinely partisan way for the interests and values of their "folks" (Mutz 2008b). This logic comes out most clearly in the United Kingdom, the United States and other adversarial two-party systems, and populists obviously thrive on this "us" and "them" discourse. However, "partisanship" is arguably also a more general logic underlying contemporary democracy (see White and Ypi 2016).

Another version of this criticism, popularized by Nassim Nicholas Taleb (2018), is that experts don't have any "skin in the game": experts give advice without bearing the negative consequences if they are wrong. Those negative consequences are instead borne by other actors, such as citizens, businesses, etc. Not only do experts thus lack incentives to provide correct advice, which makes them unreliable as advisors (see also Chapter 4). This asymmetry – that experts shape policies while others bear the risks of those policies – is also a democratic problem. It is, for instance, often claimed that experts have liberal views on immigration and border policy because they themselves do not feel the negative consequences of increased immigration, such as unemployment, increased wage competition, unsafe neighborhoods and pressure on welfare systems and social services.

9 Expertization leads to depoliticization

Expertization may also distort other features of democratic politics many will consider essential, such as the role of opinion in contrast to truth or evidence (Arendt 1968) or of contestation and conflict (Fawcett et al. 2017). Delegation to expert bodies entails insulating policy-making from political debate and strife – that is, depoliticization – and to convert political issues into questions that can be handled by "neutral" experts. The maybe clearest example is how the setting of monetary policy has been taken out of the political arena and delegated to economic experts in independent central banks. Another example is the common criticism of the EU as a depoliticization machine, which turns any political issue into technical questions to be handled by independent expert bodies that are beyond the reach of member states and regular citizens. Similar concerns have been raised about the trend toward "agencification" of regulatory issues, where important public responsibilities and much of the more detailed formulation of laws and regulations have been delegated to powerful semi-independent agencies that operate at arm's length from the elected government.

Not seldom, depoliticization can be hard to detect, because political questions, for instance, regarding the distribution of economic burdens or decision procedures, are presented as purely "technical" questions. We discussed the slippery slope from fact- to value-based judgments in Chapter 1. Other cases of depoliticization are extremely explicit. For instance, one would usually consider ethical questions related to stem-cell research, artificial intelligence and the distribution of vaccines the preserve of democratic politics. Yet, both at the national and European levels, these questions have increasingly been depoliticized through the growing reliance on ethics advisory bodies made up of philosophers and others considered to have "ethics expertise" (Littoz-Monnet 2020). Here, what we see is not experts selected for their factual and technical knowledge who then take it on themselves to also advise on ought-issues, but rather experts explicitly asked to advise on ought-issues due to their moral expertise (see Chapter 1).

This extensive role in governments for delegated expertise, whether this expertise is technical, moral or both, is criticized from many corners for distorting our ideas of what democracy is, and of what experts can deliver. Tellingly, Sheila Jasanoff (1998) has referred to the expanding field of independent regulatory agencies with considerable power as "the fifth branch of government", a branch that systematically makes the error of reducing the culturally framed ethical and political issues at the center of health, environmental and technology policy into technical issues of regulation and management. Recently, she has pursued a similar line of critique in an analysis of 18 countries' handling of the pandemic (Jasanoff et al. 2021), where "taking politics out of policy" and the failure to recognize how "measures are always value-laden" are among the key "fallacies" of many governments.

10 Experts are sheltered from elite circulation

Finally, even if one grants a role for elites in democracy (for a classical statement, see Schumpeter [1942] 1985), there is the worry that expertization may hamper processes of elite selection and circulation vital to good democratic governance. The problem may be that academic experts and professionals lack a social constituency and that the circulation in and out of governing expert communities is comparably low. Whereas leaders of political parties and interest groups in democracies change as a result of political mobilization or elections, experts in bureaucracies and advisory bodies tend to be sheltered from political pressures. Top bureaucrats and professors with specialist competence on policy issues that are key for governance may be in positions of power for many years, even decades. Heads of central banks and the bureaucratic leadership of ministries of finance or health may outlive several prime ministers and grand shifts in interest constellations and mobilization patterns in civil society.

To be sure, shielding experts and ensuring a long-term horizon for their work helps preserve their independence and ability to speak truth to power and may improve their contribution to the epistemic quality of policy development and reform. There is, for instance, plenty of evidence of a positive relationship between unpoliticized bureaucracies and expert bodies sheltered from shifting electoral outcomes, low corruption and quality of government (Rothstein 2011). But an unfortunate side effect can be that experts in positions of considerable power are unresponsive and resistant to change. A well-known example is how British top-level civil servants and expert advisors who for decades and even centuries were recruited from the arts and humanities at Oxford and Cambridge, were ill prepared and lacked elementary scientific literacy and insight into public risk construction and perceptions during the mad cow disease in the 1990s. In a sheltered system of recruitment, socialization and cultivation of skills, there were few incentives from the outside for bureaucrats and government experts to adapt their analyses and priorities to an agenda with new environmental problems and public demands for lay participation and transparency. Other examples are accusations against established governmental expertise of lagging behind in their approach to the digital economy or to institutionalized racism, as a result of conservative recruitment patterns and static expert cultures systematically shielded from public opinion and societal conflicts.

All the points on this list are potentially serious. Democratic worries are not only raised by populists, but by a range of other voices as well. It is also a mistake to assume, as those who defend and embrace expertization frequently maintain, that there is no reason for democratic concern as long as there are free and fair elections and power is delegated to experts according to democratic procedures.

At the same time, democratic concerns should not be overstated. Most would grant that democracies also should deliver knowledge-based policies, and if so expert bodies are vital. And those who believe that democracy or the "wisdom of the many" will outperform epistocracy, have yet to succeed in substantiating the claim that "pure" democracy will outperform democracies that allow for a range of expert arrangements. Also, even if there are good reasons to take the worries we have listed in this chapter seriously, there are also many examples of how democratic deliberation and decision-making can profit from expert advice. Whether democracy and expertise can be married, or whether expert arrangements will hamper and pervert democracy, depends decisively on institutional design. Hence, if we as democrats are worried about expertization, yet recognize the fact of expertise, our efforts should be channeled, not only critically "against" expertise (and "for" democratization), but also constructively into better organizing expert arrangements and political systems.

6   Designing expert bodies

A systemic perspective

We started this book with the coronavirus crisis. And while the pandemic at the time of writing seems to be over for now (although some experts caution us against letting our guard down), questions about governments' handling of the crisis will be with us for years to come. Were governments prepared for a global pandemic, and did they respond well when the crisis arose? Were the selected strategies and policies adequate? Could and should governments have performed better? Many countries and international organizations have published extensive evaluation reports of the pandemic response, and a key point under consideration is the role of expert communities and expert advice during the crisis.

Arguably, Covid-19 exposed the fact of expertise to most of us. Confronted with a global pandemic, we inevitably depend on experts and expert knowledge to make sensible and effective policies. There are few traces in these reports of the bashing of expertise that has been heard in recent years, be it in populist discourse or in some academic circles. Still, the reports put the role and recommendations from experts under critical scrutiny, and in line with what he have suggested in the previous chapters, the criticism is in part epistemic, in part democratic. The reports document instances of group think, overconfidence and disciplinary biases among expert advisors. For instance, the evaluation report from the Dutch Safety Board argues that the government's reliance on an expert advisory body dominated by medical doctors focused the attention on the situation in hospitals, while the consequences for care homes, schools, culture and businesses were ignored (Dutch Safety Board 2022). However, the reports also criticize the extensive amount of delegation of policy- and decision-making to executives and experts, in particular within the public health domain. This, it is argued, contributed to a marginalization of the political role of parliaments and to a depoliticization of issues and priorities that are genuinely political.

DOI: 10.4324/9781003106555-7

This line of critique against the extensive powers delegated to public health authorities in particular during the first phase of the pandemic is, for instance, pursued in both the Danish and Norwegian evaluation reports (Folketinget 2021; NOU 2021).

These criticisms raise the question of whether there are better ways to design expert bodies and the relationship between such bodies and the other parts of a political system. The coronavirus crisis gave this question novel urgency. Yet, considering the massive expert dependency of modern societies and policy-making, the importance of this issue goes far beyond the role of experts during the pandemic. Given the fact of expertise on the one hand, and the range of reasonable epistemic and democratic concerns over the political role of experts on the other, how should expert advice and the surrounding public institutions of contemporary democracies be designed? In other words: are there ways to institutionalize expertise that address worries about expertization?

In this concluding chapter, we further pursue the ambition to combine arguments from discussions in philosophy with real-world examples and lessons from empirical scholarship. We fully share the concern of Rainer Forst, who has noted how normative political theory and empirical studies of politics in recent years "have lost touch with each other" and "developed languages of their own" (Forst 2021, see also Pedersen 2009). Our aim is to give practical recommendations about the design of institutions, but with the philosophical and conceptual arguments developed in previous chapters as backdrop.

We also take as our point of departure what we previously have referred to as "a deliberative systems" approach. This view implies that the political system as a whole is expected to ensure that public deliberation can improve political decision-making, and that there is a division of labor between different parts of the system in achieving different essential functions in a democracy. On this basis, we distinguish between three types of measures that are essential to ensure experts' epistemic performance: those that target experts' *behavior*, their *judgments* and the *organization* of expert bodies and advice. We give examples of promising measures that are already in place and also suggest how existing mechanisms may be designed better.

However, as we have seen, the worries about the political role of experts are also democratic, and we go on to discuss how such worries most adequately could be addressed. We show, first, that measures to ensure expert bodies' epistemic credentials may have important democratic credentials as well. Second, there are ways to "democratize expertise" (Weingart 2005; see also Krick and Holst 2020, Krick 2021), and we review different strategies for doing so. We contend that such democratization may be important to alleviate democratic concerns; yet it should be pursued only if, and in ways that, do not decrease expert bodies' epistemic credentials (Holst and Molander 2017, Gundersen and Holst 2022). Third, the depth and range of democratic worries obviously cannot be addressed properly without considering other parts of the political system: it follows from the systemic approach that worries about expertization cannot be alleviated exclusively through proper design and redesign of expert bodies. We show and give examples of how this is the case with several of the democratic worries. But also epistemic concerns over experts' performance will not be sufficiently addressed by a simpleminded focus on the internal norms and features of expert communities.

The epistemic function of expert arrangements

We outlined in Chapter 3 how Jane Mansbridge and colleagues (2012, 11–12) conceptualize democratic polities as "deliberative systems". Public deliberation fulfills three different functions in such systems: the epistemic function of producing "preferences, opinions and decisions that are appropriately informed by facts and logic", and "the outcome of substantive and meaningful consideration of relevant reasons"; the ethical function of promoting "mutual respect among citizens" and the democratic function of promoting "an inclusive process of collective choice". All functions are equally decisive for the overall system to have normative legitimacy, but, importantly, individual institutions must not fulfill all three functions equally well. The idea is rather to develop an adequate division of labor where epistemic, ethical and democratic deficits in one part of the system can be compensated for in other parts of the system.

Also, from this systemic perspective, some institutions may have one of the functions as their primary function, or some functions may be more decisive in some organizations and institutional contexts than in others (Mansbridge et al. 2012; see also Parkinson 2018). For instance, broad participation is important in civil society and the public sphere, while the supreme court or the central bank and a range of agencies are non-majoritarian and predominantly meritocratic institutions; the adherence to norms of mutual respect is important in the deliberations of parliaments but do not apply to the same degree in quarrels on Facebook; and standards of facts and logic are crucial in the academic community but less so at a party rally.

Generally, the primary rationale for expert arrangements is to fulfill an epistemic function. Expertise is supposed to be an epistemic "filter" in the making of laws and policies (Christiano 2012). This does not imply that democratic and ethical functions are irrelevant when considering the political role of experts – as we saw in Chapter 5. It does however imply that the focus should be on the extent to which epistemic communities are epistemically trustworthy and on whether the design of expert bodies increases the likelihood of providing us with decisions and policies that are "truth-sensitive" and based on "facts and logic". It also implies that measures to ensure and cultivate democratic credentials must be made and shaped in ways that do not weaken the epistemic credentials of expert arrangements.

Measures to ensure expert performance

As mentioned, we can distinguish between three types of measures that are important to ensure the primary epistemic function of expert advice and expert bodies (Molander 2016, Ch. 4, Holst and Molander 2017; see also Keohane, Lane and Oppenheimer 2014, Moore 2017, 2021, Parkhurst 2017).

Expert behavior

The first set of measures pertains to experts' *behavior* as inquirers. Generally, proper experts operate in accordance with epistemic norms. This can be the norms that we know from the scientific ethos (cf. Merton's [1942] 1973 classical formulation of the CUDOS-system; for a revision, see Longino 2002, see also Tranøy 1976 on "norms of inquiry"). But it can also be versions of this ethos that are tailored to the advisory context (e.g. Pielke 2007 on the "honest broker"; see also Collins and Evans 2007, Gundersen 2018), and so emphasize additional requirements such as an orientation toward consensus, communicability toward nonexpert audiences, and clarity about uncertainties. The adherence to such norms is often presupposed when political authorities and citizens appeal to science and expertise or seek advice or even delegate decisions to different groups of experts: the reasonable assumption is that experts, when they behave like experts are supposed to, feel bound and obliged by epistemic norms, the most basic being the obligation to truth and justification.

Of course, when governments decide to establish an expert commission or a specialized agency, they may have a mixed set of reasons. Beside a genuine motivation to solve policy problems based on the best available knowledge, decision-makers may call on experts for symbolic and strategic reasons. Yet, an expert commission that disregards epistemic norms will easily lose its authority and privileged status, for instance, if the scientific community raises concerns about the quality of its arguments. Similarly, an environmental or health agency that regularly delivers sloppy analyses and recommendations without a proper basis in knowledge will often be of little use to politicians who seek to back their political priorities and strategies with "evidence".

Yet, in addition, measures can be taken to increase the likelihood that experts behave according to an epistemic ethos. Investigatory procedures can be spelled out in regulations and guidelines which specify, for instance, that expert advice should be based on research and other validated knowledge, or that experts should reach their conclusions through deliberation. There can also be procedures for sanctioning sloppy work, and for excluding experts with bad records or with a stake in the matter from reassignment. Such guidelines and procedures are often lacking or extremely rudimentary, even in the case of well-established expert arrangements. The regulations of Norwegian expert commissions, for instance, highlight how commissions must answer their terms of reference and make reports based on systematic and relevant arguments, adequate "knowledge" and "expertise", etc. However, the guidelines do not specify any special role for science and research (see Holst and Molander 2018). The responsible ministry is not required to involve academics or to check the training, background, achievements, interests, affiliations, etc. of academics before selecting them. There is also no code of conduct stating responsibilities and standards of good expert behavior.

In contrast, the European Commission operates with a rather detailed set of epistemic parameters in its approach to expert advice (Metz 2015). Processual requirements for "expert enquiries" and "scientific assessments" are spelled out quite minutely: when possible, investigations should be pursued in a "scientific" manner based on "rigorous methods for testing hypothetical explanations of natural or social facts and systems"; experts should generally and clearly "highlight the evidence (e.g. sources, references) upon which they base their advice, as well as any persisting uncertainty and divergent views"; and policymakers should strive for "impartiality" and "neutrality" in their take-up and avoid "just listening to one side of the argument or of particular groups getting privileged access" (European Commission 2002, 12). The same goes for procedures of expert selection, where primary concerns include achieving "scientific excellence", as endorsed by "the judgement of peers", and "taking account of indicators such as the number and impact of refereed publications" (European Commission 2002, 9). Generally, expert group "members shall be selected in a transparent manner" and "on the basis of clearly defined objective criteria", and "departments shall maintain a record of the process including the terms of reference and the main contributions of different experts or groups of experts" (European Commission 2002, 12). Another concern is "to minimize the risk of vested interests distorting the advice": experts are to "commit themselves to act independently and in the public interest" and shall be informed that they may be "excluded from the group or a specific meeting ... should a conflict of interest arise" (European Commission 2010, 10).

As we will return to, the actual practice of expert bodies may look very different from the practices outlined in formal guidelines and procedures. Guidelines may look more advanced on paper than they are in practice, and sometimes even function as window dressing for serious malfunctions (see, e.g. Littoz-Monnet 2020). Good practice is moreover not necessarily codified: an expert body may conduct the most rigorous of reviews, even if its procedures are not elaborated on in any detail on paper. Still, explicit requirements clarify expectations and the basis on which experts can be criticized for not behaving like good experts are supposed to.

Expert judgments

The second set of measures target the *judgments* of experts. To ensure epistemic performance, experts need to be held accountable, in the sense that they can be called "to account" for their judgments. Accountability, according to Mark Bovens, is

> a relationship between an actor and a forum, in which the actor has an obligation to explain and to justify his or her conduct, and in which the forum can pose questions and pass judgment, and the actor may face consequences.
> (Bovens 2007, 450; Bovens et al. 2014)

The most obvious forum for testing expert judgments and detecting fallacies and biases is the forum of immediate peers: economists being questioned by other economists, medical experts being scrutinized by other medical experts, etc. This kind of peer review is deeply institutionalized in the scientific community, where the arguments and analyses presented in academic articles are reviewed and criticized by peers before being published. The important function of academic peer review for public policy even caught the public eye during the coronavirus pandemic. The rapid spread and mutation of the virus led to an urgent need for up-to-date knowledge and a constant flow of new research, yet experts cautioned decision-makers against basing policy decisions on results from studies that had not yet been through peer review.

In many cases, there are good reasons to have expert judgments and arguments reviewed by academics from other disciplines, too. Experts in other fields bring a different perspective to the problem and therefore may be able to spot biases and faulty assumptions. This is, for instance, the routine procedure of SAPEA – Science Advice for Policy by European Academies[1] – when draft reports, on topics ranging from sustainable food systems to energy transition and aging populations, are sent out for comment to reviewers within different relevant fields and disciplines. Another European-level example is the European Commission's Regulatory Scrutiny Board (European Commission 2022). This is an accountability body that checks the quality of the Commission's impact assessments and policy evaluations, which are usually based on studies commissioned from consultancies or research institutes. The board can issue a positive or negative opinion on an impact assessment. In case of a negative opinion, the impact assessment must be reviewed and resubmitted. This kind of scrutiny body may raise red flags when policy proposals are not based on sound knowledge, for instance, if an impact assignment is based on a sloppy consultancy study. This may also encourage the administration to assess the impact of a policy proposal more thoroughly and external knowledge suppliers to raise the quality of their work. Yet, it is noteworthy that the members of the Board are mostly economists, and likely that this will shape their assessments of regulatory quality (compared to assessments made by a board where, for instance, political scientists and lawyers play a greater role).

Reports from governmental advisory commissions in the Nordic countries are regularly sent out for scrutiny in broad hearing processes. Experts and expert communities often use this opportunity to give input and air criticism, for instance, if the reports are conceived to have disciplinary biases and leave out important insights from other relevant research areas. Two recent reports from Norwegian advisory commissions provide good examples. During the hearing after the launch of a report from the Drug Policy Commission, research environments within public health and psychiatry without representation around the commission table criticized the report for leaving out or misinterpreting medical research that emphasizes the harms of drug use (Pedersen et al. 2021). Similarly, a recent commission report on gender differences in school performance authored by researchers and professors from public health, economics and the experimentalist branch of educational science was criticized during the hearing process for leaving out essential perspectives from sociology and gender studies. At the same time, critics have described these hearing inputs from competing research environments and disciplines as "unscientific" and lacking in rigor and called for a stricter multi-disciplinary review process, supplementing the traditional hearing procedures.

Epistemic considerations may also speak in favor of putting expert judgments under review in broader fora. This can, for instance, be fora where expert judgments are confronted with bureaucrats' knowledge of what is administratively feasible, or where competent stakeholders can scrutinize the claims and recommendations of experts based on their insights into what works on the ground (Heclo 1974, Gornitzka and Sverdrup 2011). The advisory commissions we find in the Nordic countries are good examples of this kind of forum. While university professors and institute researchers have come to play an increasingly important role on advisory commissions in some Nordic countries (Norway and Denmark), civil servants and interest groups still have a massive presence. In all the Nordic countries, civil servants are present on nearly all advisory commissions (80–100 percent), and interest groups participate on a large majority of commissions everywhere but in Sweden (Christensen et al. 2022). The same goes for the European Commission's expert group system, where 80 percent of expert groups have participants from national administrative bodies, whereas interest groups/societal actors are present on 40 percent of expert groups and scientists are present on about one third of bodies (Gornitzka and Sverdrup 2011). Nordic-style hearing procedures also have the function of exposing expert advice to input from a broader range of actors. In particular in cases of extensive commission reports that deal with politically salient issues, such as welfare state, labor market or public sector reform, there are sometimes several hundred written hearing inputs. These mostly come from civil society and professional organizations, ministries, agencies and municipalities, which review the reports' analyses and recommendations. This adds to the detailed consultation procedures within the government administration both before commissions are established, and after their reports are delivered, and the commissions' consultations with key stakeholders, organizations and the social partners during their proceedings.

Finally, the parliament or the public sphere at large may serve as accountability fora and contribute to improving the epistemic quality of expert advice. This is particularly important when the knowledge basis developed by the executive is narrow and central issues have been swept under the carpet. Critics have claimed that this happened in the case of the Transatlantic Trade and Investment Partnership (TTIP) in the EU.

The European Parliament's scrutiny and criticism of the information and analyses developed by the European Commission regarding TTIP arguably contributed decisively to a more enlightened process (Rosén and Tørnblad 2018). Parliaments, but also the media and public debate, played a similar role in many countries both in revisions of corona policies that turned out to have important downsides, and in the post hoc evaluations of policies and strategies. Traditional media and increasingly also social media have been labeled "the fourth branch" of government/"the fourth estate", and this branch obviously plays an important democratic role. However, critical journalism and media exposure may also be key to reveal unfortunate and even devastating, foreseen or unforeseen, effects of policies and may have a no less important function as an accountability mechanism and epistemic check.

Also social movements, public intellectuals, organizational representatives and participants in public debate can take on such a function. Consider, for example, the significant role of the feminist movement in making public policies better for all, irrespective of gender and sexuality. Accountability fora with broad participation of citizens can also be designed and established alongside existing arrangements and institutions. Hélène Landemore (2020) proposes crowdsourcing measures and deliberative mini-publics to strengthen epistemic scrutiny in democracies, but also recommends that parliaments should be equipped with a second chamber that consists of a representative sample of the citizenry drawn by lottery.

In both such inclusive accountability fora, and in fora with more limited participation, scientists and specialists can be asked to account for critical assumptions, explain models used, specify their limits and present alternative models (see Schlefer 2012, 280–281). This is what happened when corona experts were pushed both by peers, and by politicians and the media, to clarify and justify their estimates and scenarios. Importantly, demands can also be put on experts to explain what they do *not* know: experts tend to be overconfident and often need to be pushed to explicate their specific area of expertise and the limits of their competence. For example, experts on engineering may have no special competence in law, and vice versa, and a technical expert in some area may lack insight into the evaluative, non-scientific dimensions of a problem. During the pandemic, we saw an increased awareness of the limitations of public health and medical expertise, even if we also depended immensely on exactly this kind of expertise during this time. This resulted in demands on the corona experts to explain in clearer terms the reach of their knowledge and the line between their expertise and their private and political preferences.

The organization of expert inquiry

The third set of measures pertains to the *organization* of expert inquiry and judgment. An obvious organizational issue is the setup of the relationship between political principals and experts. Political control over experts can pervert truth-seeking, for example, when contracted scientists are asked to work on narrow, politically biased mandates, or along with political appointees with pre-set views and limited relevant expertise (Oreskes 2019). Research has shown that politicians and bureaucrats can use various ex ante and ex post mechanisms to steer the work of expert groups, including through the selection of experts and through the participation of ministry bureaucrats as commission members and secretaries (Hesstvedt and Christensen 2021). There is thus a need to organize the relationship between decision-makers and expert advisors in a way that ensures autonomous, un-politicized expert inquiries (see also Dowding and Taflaga 2020). Efforts to mitigate politicization and ensure independent expert deliberations can target the levers principals have for controlling experts. This can be done, for instance, through greater transparency or a more formalized procedure for the selection of experts, by staffing commission secretariats with independent experts rather than ministry officials, or by establishing clearer rules barring civil servants serving on commissions from representing the interests of their department.

Other aspects of how expert bodies are organized are vital as well. For one thing, psychological research suggests that it matters significantly whether experts work on their own or in groups. Experts reasoning alone are known to be exposed to "confirmation bias" and other biases, whereas deliberating groups are less prone to these fallacies and may enlarge the pool of ideas and information and weed out bad arguments (Mercier 2011). This may speak against "one-man committees" that are sometimes used, for instance, in the Swedish committee system.

Yet, the positive epistemic effects of deliberation also depend crucially on diversity (Kitcher 1990, Mercier 2011). Without diversity, deliberation may work in the opposite direction and create groupthink (Sunstein and Hastie 2015). It is thus crucial to organize expert work along team and deliberative lines and to provide for necessary diversity and exposure to criticism from wider circles (see also Moore and MacKenzie 2020). This makes disciplinarity diversity within expert groups paramount. For instance, an expert group giving advice on social security policy should arguably include both economists and other social scientists, medical scientists and lawyers. Similarly, a commission investigating the government's handling of a terrorist attack may need experts on terrorism and policing, but also legal expertise and specialists on public policy and administration.

While this idea of disciplinary diversity is straightforward enough on paper, and increasingly embraced in regulatory guidelines and best practice manuals, it is often not followed in practice. Academic disciplines tend to fiercely protect their "turf" or jurisdiction over certain policy issues, and often find the inclusion of experts from other disciplines a nuisance that makes it difficult to reason clearly and to reach agreement. Many scientific advisory bodies set up to advise government on the coronavirus response were composed almost exclusively of medical experts, who were reluctant to give access to other types of experts. For instance, the Dutch government's principal expert advice mechanism during the handling of the pandemic – the Outbreak Management Team (OMT) – was made up of about 40 medical experts, and actively fended off calls for including experts from other fields such as behavioral psychology or economics. Similarly, the expert commission appointed by the French President Macron to examine the big challenges of inequality, climate and ageing was composed of 26 economists but no one from any other discipline. When asked about the composition of the commission, one of its chairmen – former IMF chief economist Olivier Blanchard – answered:

> When setting up a commission of this type, you have to choose whether to open it up to civil society or to other specialists, such as sociologists. We have decided to stick to economists, knowing that our work will be one of the sources of reflection among others that the president will have.
>
> (quoted in Madeline and Charrel 2020, own translation)

In addition to disciplinary diversity, the inclusion of actors with other types of knowledge – regulatory competence, local knowledge, experience-based expertise, etc. that contribute to a fuller understanding of a political problem and how to address it – may be important. We have already mentioned the hybrid Nordic-style committees, and there are similar hybrid committees and advisory groups in many countries and in international organizations, from the European Commission's expert groups to the many mixed working and expert groups under the different organizations, departments and offices of the UN. We can zoom in on almost any UN organization, for instance, UN Women or UN's Children's Fund (UNICEF), and find a complex structure of variably composed expert groups and consultation procedures.

Finally, social and political pluralism may contribute to the epistemic pluralism that we know is decisive for deliberative quality. A group consisting of people with varying social and cultural backgrounds is *prima facie* likely to produce a larger and more diverse pool of arguments regarding some issue than a socially and culturally homogenous group. To the extent that this is the case, it speaks for pluralism in expert bodies in terms of gender, social, geographical and ethnic backgrounds, and for quota policies or other preferential treatment measures to ensure it; out of concerns for democratic representativeness, but arguably also for epistemic reasons (Holst and Langvatn 2021).

From the perspective of diversity, it also seems important that advisory committees and other expert arrangements include experts with varying political views and value commitments. Despite this, we often see expert committees where experts share normative orientations. Yet, in some cases, governments also seek to include diverse political perspectives in expert advice. A good example is the US Presidential Commission on the Supreme Court set up by President Biden to examine the politically explosive question of reforms of the US Supreme Court, which deliberately included academics from across the political spectrum. Ensuring value diversity among expert advisors may be a way to ensure democratic legitimacy. Commissions where experts look politically cherry-picked will easily lose authority. Yet, there is also an epistemic argument against expert arrangements consisting purely of like-minded individuals, as more politically diverse expert groups may come up with a broader range of ideas and avoid ideological biases in the treatment of a problem.

Democratization of expertise

It must be emphasized that even when all or most of these mechanisms are more or less in place, this does not guarantee that experts pick the better policies and make the right judgments. Policy- and decision-making in contemporary societies is characterized by limited knowledge, complexity and uncertainty, and even the best package of measures cannot completely rule out expert biases and mistakes. Yet, to the extent that the mechanisms we have suggested in fact target the sources of experts' failures and bad practices effectively, and so address our epistemic worries, they increase the likelihood of improved policy- and decision quality, or at least, decreases the chance of "misrule" (see Elster 2013 on the "negative" approach to institutional design; Holst and Christensen 2022).

But what about the democratic worries? Indeed, even if we take it that the function of expert arrangements is primarily epistemic, we have argued that the democratic worries about expertization enumerated in Chapter 5 are all worthy of serious consideration. Also, since a political system should fulfill both democratic and ethical functions in addition to having epistemic credentials, the design of expert arrangements should contribute to fulfilling these functions as well, even if there can be cases where clear epistemic benefits may outbalance some democratic losses.

Peter Weingart (2005, 53–54) has argued that "democratizing expertise" can be achieved (1) by taking relevant lay knowledge into account in the production of knowledge, (2) by giving laypeople access to expert knowledge, (3) by granting laypeople access to experts and (4) by allowing laypeople to have some influence on the selection of experts. We have in effect introduced both (1) and (3) already in the measures outlined earlier for addressing epistemic worries. We touched upon (1), for instance, when we argued that the cognitive diversity of expert bodies when needed should include stakeholder and local knowledge and lay perspectives, and in our outline of the role of accountability fora with broad participation. We introduced (3) when we argued for consultation procedures that bring experts and non-experts into interchange. Yet, our approach above was epistemic: relevant lay knowledge should be taken into account and laypeople should be granted access to experts to the extent that it brings in new perspectives, enriches the pool of arguments and sharpens deliberations in ways that are likely to contribute to better policies and decisions.

Here we turn to the democratic rationale for these measures: including lay knowledge and providing access to experts can also contribute to decreased political alienation, to make deliberations more public, to shift power from the unelected to the elected, etc. In other words, these measures can generally address the worries of both proceduralists and epistemic democrats, since it may contribute both to the realization of democratic ideals of political equality and self-government, and to the utilization of the perceived "wisdom of crowds". This highlights how democratic and epistemic concerns in the best of cases can pull in the same direction, and there are many examples from the real world of advisory mechanisms and expert bodies where provision of specialized knowledge, an investigatory ethos, peer review, expert autonomy and institutional independence go together with participatory credentials (Krick and Holst 2020, Krick, Christensen and Holst 2019, Krick 2021).

However, Weingart also mentions other ways of democratizing expertise. For one thing, laypeople can be given access to expert knowledge (2). A precondition for such access is transparency, by now perceived as a gold standard of good governance. Expert reports and expert advice can be made public. Background documents and report drafts can be published as well, after the report has been launched, or earlier in the process. During the corona crisis, we saw tremendous variation among countries on this point. Where some governments opted for radical transparency and exposed the full knowledge basis of policy choices to the public, exposing often considerable expert disagreement, others opted for secrecy and top-down instructions to the public. Another transparency measure is to make meeting minutes from expert proceedings public. This is standard, for instance, in the expert group system of the European Commission. Alternatively, the meetings can be opened up to the public, for instance, by means of digital broadcasting, or engaged citizens, stakeholders and journalists may be invited to be physically present to observe and report.

In addition to transparency, other measures could be taken to ensure laypeople access to expert knowledge. An interesting example is how some parliaments have established units of "legislative science advice", whether a committee (such as France's OPECST), an office (such as the UK Parliamentary Office of Science and Technology) or an institute (such as the Rathenau Institute in the Netherlands) that produce review reports of available research and evidence on topics that are on the parliamentary agenda (Akerlof et al. 2019, Geddes 2021). This increases the possibilities for legislators to consult expertise and to anchor their proposals and deliberations in up-to-date knowledge for instance on policy and regulatory effects.

Moreover, laypeople can have influence on the selection of experts – Weingart's strategy (4). This is the case, for instance, when expert groups are established not by ministries and agencies, but by parliaments. Another example is how the selection of representatives from civil society to expert committees is delegated to the civil society organizations and interest groups themselves.

Once more, these strategies of democratizing expert arrangements serve both democratic and epistemic purposes, at least under fortunate circumstances. Transparency measures, expert commissions composed by parliamentarians or based on input from civil society, and policies to ensure social and political diversity in expert bodies and accountability fora may all contribute to exposing and mitigating expert biases and mistakes, and enable investigations and deliberations that are richer, sharper and better. These mechanisms and measures may at the same time contribute to reducing the different democratic worries about expertization: increasing the role of the elected, citizens and civil society in politics, exposing undue depoliticization of political issues, reducing citizen disaffection with politics and so on.

Finally, they may very well, and in the best of cases, be compatible with the ethical function as well. The systems approach to public deliberation emphasizes the importance of mutual respect, in addition to fulfillment of democratic and epistemic functions, and there is a range of examples of how deliberations both within highly performing expert bodies, and between expert communities and citizens, take place in uncondescending and appropriately respectful ways.

Still, there are also tensions between epistemic, democratic and ethical concerns that we need to consider when we establish and reform expert arrangements (Holst and Molander 2017, Gundersen and Holst 2022). Or to put it differently: expert bodies and expert advice may be designed so as to have democratic and ethical merits, but end up scoring poorly from the perspective of epistemic standards. Democratizing by means of including lay knowledge in expert advice may in the best of cases contribute to correcting expert biases, but it can also result in undue and disproportional consideration of arguments that are irrelevant, obviously invalid or fleshed out in more accurate terms in expert contributions. Making expert knowledge public for citizens to scrutinize can improve validity; flaws in expert reasoning can be identified; omissions can be detected. However, due to epistemic asymmetries, lay monitoring is a persistent source of fallacies and biases as well (see Pincione and Teson 2006 on "discourse failure"). Transparency can moreover result in public and media exposure with a chilling effect on experts' inquiries. This endangers deliberative and decision quality, for instance, if such exposure makes experts avoid raising controversial and unpopular views (see Chambers 2004 on "deliberations behind closed doors"), or results in increased pressures from lobby groups (Gundersen and Holst 2022).

Similar considerations arguably apply when citizens are included in expert deliberations – for instance, in expert committees, in consultation or accountability fora, or through crowdsourcing – and when they are involved in the selection of experts, be it directly, for instance, if parliamentarians review candidates for expert positions, or indirectly, for instance, when such selection processes are topics of media debate. Also in these cases, the novice/expert problem may occur (Goldman 2001): different types of non-expert political actors may try to assess experts' merits, explanations and analyses, but due to epistemic asymmetries, they are not really in an epistemic position to do so.

As for the democratization strategy of increasing the social and political pluralism among experts, epistemic asymmetry is not the major challenge if the selected experts have competence in relevant domains (while it naturally may be a challenge if they don't). The important question rather is the extent to which measures to increase the descriptive representation of some group contribute to the increased cognitive diversity that is so decisive from the perspective of epistemic outcomes. Surely, there are cases where, for instance, gender quotas or geographical representation is likely to expand the amount of perspectives and universe of relevant arguments, for instance, in an expert commission on sexual violence or regional development. Yet, in other cases, ensuring disciplinary or methodological diversity will be much more important for the quality of expert deliberations (see Holst and Langvatn 2021 for an analysis of the costs and benefits of descriptive representation).

Finally, epistemic norms and norms of civility do overlap to a large extent. Yet, they are also different and in possible tension. Taking arguments seriously means to take a stance on them, and too much politeness could cover up significant intellectual disagreements and disputes and reduce the quality of discourse. Consequently, respect codes in deliberations among experts would typically be less strict and less comprehensive than similar codes in, for example, parliamentary settings.

In these less straightforward cases, where there may be tensions and conflicts between ethical, democratic and epistemic demands, the design of expert bodies and expert advice should prioritize measures with a firm epistemic justification, given expert arrangements' primary function, and avoid measures that may have democratic and ethical credentials, but with poor epistemic credentials.

Measures in other parts of the system

In the political system at large, ensuring the epistemic function is of course no more important than ensuring the democratic and ethical functions. Our systemic perspective implies that we must consider not only how expert arrangements may be designed so they better mitigate epistemic and democratic worries, but also the extent to which such worries may be more adequately and better addressed by targeting other parts of the system.

No doubt, exclusively focusing on the design of expert bodies to minimize expert biases and mistakes and maximize their performance, will not do. Experts' adherence to epistemic norms is, for instance, likely to depend decisively on the long-term cultivation of well-functioning expert cultures and their professional socialization in education systems. Whether or not our experts are equipped to speak truth to power, steer clear of arrogant and condescending attitudes, and rank epistemic concerns above their personal interests when they operate as experts is linked to their deeper mindset and understanding of their societal and political role. This reflects the internal norms and regulations of expert communities, but ultimately also broader cultural norms, and the discourse in media, among politicians and in the public sphere, in school and local communities.

We are moreover more likely to end up with highly performing experts when experts are recruited from a society where there are equal opportunities, and no groups are systematically excluded from proper consideration because of their social background, gender or minority status. This connects the epistemic performance of expert communities intimately to the organization of society and public institutions at large. The role of the broader system becomes even more decisive when our concern is not only experts' performance, but eventually decision and policy quality, which is the concern that motivates our efforts to mitigate epistemic worries about expertization in the first place. An expert committee composed of our finest experts will not contribute to better policies if its report and advice are simply disregarded, and even the highest expert achievements will not make much difference in a "post truth" political system where politicians and citizens systematically ignore what experts are saying.

We will similarly be unable to address the democratic worries about expertization without considering the fuller range of public institutions; simply "democratizing expertise" will not do. Whether or not citizens experience political alienation depends on the extent of expertization and how experts behave, but it is also related to educational and socioeconomic inequalities, and to whether politicians and civil society organizations are able to establish public discourses that make people feel more at home in the world. Counteracting the technocratic, depoliticized image of politics is partly the responsibility of experts and a concern when we design our expert bodies, but also requires broader efforts and a change in discourse among all political actors. Giving experts and elites generally "skin in the game" on par with ordinary citizens is likely to require distributive and educational policies to reduce differences between elites and non-elites. If there is too much parliamentary delegation of agenda setting and decision-making to expert bodies, this problem must primarily be addressed by the parliaments themselves and cannot be mitigated by this or the other measure to democratize expert deliberations.

To conclude, when designing expert arrangements, political equality and citizens' ability to see themselves as taking part in a project of self-government are genuine concerns that must be taken seriously. Still, as expertise is a "fact", and the primary function of expert arrangements is epistemic, "democratization of expertise" cannot be the principal solution to these challenges. Rather, reforms of expert bodies need to address both epistemic and democratic worries, and representative and participatory concerns should only be pursued in ways that do not hurt expert bodies' epistemic credentials, and can in many cases more effectively be ensured in other parts of the political system.

Note

1 SAPEA and the Group of Chief Scientific Advisors make up the European Commission's Scientific Advice Mechanism.

References

Abbott, A. (1988). *The System of Professions. An Essay on the Division of Expert Labor*. Chicago: Chicago University Press.

Achen, C.H., & Bartels, L.M. (2016). *Democracy for Realists: Why Elections Do Not Produce Responsive Government*. Princeton, NJ: Princeton University Press.

Akerlof, G.A., & Schiller, R.J. (2009). *Animal Spirits. How Human Psychology Drives the Economy, and Why It Matters for Global Capitalism*. Princeton, NJ: Princeton University Press.

Akerlof, K., Tyler, C., Foxen, S. E., Heath, E., Gual Soler, M., Allegra, A., ... & Yarime, M. (2019). A collaboratively derived international research agenda on legislative science advice. *Palgrave Communications*, 5(1), 1–13.

Albareda, A. (2020). Prioritizing professionals? How the democratic and professionalized nature of interest groups shapes their degree of access to EU officials. *European Political Science Review*, 12(4), 485–501.

Alexandrova, A. (2017). *A Philosophy for the Science of Well-Being*. Oxford: Oxford University Press.

Alexiadou, D., & Gunaydin, H. (2019). Commitment or expertise? Technocratic appointments as political responses to economic crises. *European Journal of Political Research*, 58(3), 845–865.

Ancell, A. (2017). Democracy isn't *that* smart (but we can make it smarter): On Landemore's Democratic Reason. *Episteme*, 14(2), 161–175.

Anderson, E. (2006). The epistemology of democracy. *Episteme*, 3(1–2), 8–22.

Angner, E. (2006). Economists as experts: Overconfidence in theory and practice. *Journal of Economic Methodology*, 13(1), 1–24.

Anton, T. (1969). Policy-making and political culture in Sweden. *Scandinavian Political Studies*, 4(A4), 88–102.

Arendt, H. (1968). Truth and politics. In H. Arendt (ed.), *Between Past and Future. Eight Exercises in Political Thought*. New York: Viking Press.

Aristotle. (1981). *Politics*. London: Penguin.

Arter, D. (2008). *Scandinavian Politics Today*. 2nd ed. Manchester: Manchester University Press.

Backer, I.L. (2013). *Loven – hvordan blir den til?* Oslo: Universitetsforlaget.

Bagehot, W. (1872). *Physics and Politics.* London: Henry S. King.

Béland, D., & Cox, R.H. (Eds.). (2010). *Ideas and Politics in Social Science Research.* Oxford: Oxford University Press.

Berger, P., & Luckman, T. (1966). *The Social Construction of Reality: A Treatise in the Sociology of Knowledge.* Harmondsworth: Penguin.

Bertsou, E. (2022). Bring in the experts? Citizen preferences for independent experts in political decision-making processes. *European Journal of Political Research*, 61(1), 255–267.

Bertram, C. (1997). Political Justification, Theoretical Complexity, and Democratic Community. *Ethics*, 107(4), 563–583.

Bertsou, E., & Caramani, D. (2022). People haven't had enough of experts: Technocratic attitudes among citizens in nine European democracies. *American Journal of Political Science*, 66(1), 5–23.

Blanchard, O., Romer, D., Spence, M., & Stiglitz, J. (2012). *In the Wake of the Crisis. Leading Economists Reassess Economic Policy.* Cambridge, MA: MIT Press.

Blichner, L., & Molander, A. (2008). Mapping juridification. *European Law Journal*, 14(1), 36–54.

Blyth, M. (2013). *Austerity: The History of a Dangerous Idea.* Oxford: Oxford University Press.

Bogner, A. (2021). *Die Epistemisierung des Politischen. Wie die Macht des Wissens die Demokratie gefährdet.* Stuttgart: Reclam.

Bohman, J. (2000). *Public Deliberation. Pluralism, Complexity, Democracy.* Cambridge, MA: MIT Press.

Boswell, C. (2008). The political functions of expert knowledge: Knowledge and legitimation in European Union immigration policy. *Journal of European Public Policy*, 15(4), 471–488.

Bouwen, P. (2002). Corporate lobbying in the European Union: The logic of access. *Journal of European Public Policy*, 9(3), 365–390.

Bovens, M. (2007). Analysing and assessing accountability: A conceptual framework. *European Law Journal*, 13(4), 447–468.

Bovens, M., Schillemans, T., & Goodin, R. (2014). Public accountability. In Bovens, M., Schillemans, T., & Goodin, R. (eds.), *The Oxford Handbook of Public Accountability* (pp. 1–22). Oxford: Oxford University Press.

Bovens, M., & Wille, A. (2017). *Diploma Democracy: The Rise of Political Meritocracy.* Oxford: Oxford University Press.

Brennan, J. (2013). Epistocracy and public reason. In A. Cudd & S. Scholz (eds.), *Philosophical Perspectives on Democracy in the Twenty-First Century* (pp. 191–204). Berlin: Springer.

Brennan, J. (2016). *Against Democracy.* Princeton, NJ: Princeton University Press.

Bressers, D., Twist, M., Steen, M., & Schulz, J. (2017). The contested autonomy of policy advisory bodies. In *Palgrave Handbook of Public Administration and Management in Europe* (pp. 1189–211). London: Palgrave Macillan.

Brown, M. (2009). *Science in Democracy. Expertise, Institutions, and Representation.* Cambridge: MIT Press.

Buchanan, A. (2004). Political liberalism and social epistemology. *Philosophy and Public Affairs*, 32(2), 95–130.

Busuioc, M., & Rimkutė, D. (2020). The promise of bureaucratic reputation approaches for the EU regulatory state. *Journal of European Public Policy*, 27(8), 1256–1269.

Bächtiger, A., Spörndli, M., Steenbergen, M.R., & Steiner, J. (2007). Deliberation in legislatures: Antecedents and outcomes. In S.W. Rosenberg (ed.), *Deliberation, Participation and Democracy. Can the People Govern?* (pp. 82–100). London: Palgrave Macmillan.

Cairney, P. (2016). *The Politics of Evidence-Based Policy Making*. London: Palgrave Macmillan.

Callon, M. (1999). The role of lay people in the production and dissemination of scientific knowledge. *Science, Technology & Society*, 4(1), 81–94.

Campbell, J.L. (2002). Ideas, politics, and public policy. *Annual Review of Sociology*, 28, 21–38.

Campbell, J.L., & Pedersen, O.K. (2014). *The National Origins of Policy Ideas*. Princeton, NJ: Princeton University Press.

Caplan, B. (2007). *The Myth of the Rational Voter: Why Democracies Choose Bad Policies*. Princeton, NJ: Princeton University Press.

Caramani, D. (2017). Will vs. reason: The populist and technocratic forms of political representation and their critique to party government. *American Political Science Review*, 111(01), 54–67.

Carpenter, D. (2010). *Reputation and Power*. Princeton, NJ: Princeton University Press.

Carr-Saunders, A. M., & Wilson, P. A. (1933). *The Professions*. London: Frank Cass.

Cerovan, I. (2020). *Epistemic Democracy and Political Legitimacy*. Cham: Palgrave Macmillan.

Chambers, S. (2004). Behind closed doors: Publicity, secrecy, and the quality of deliberation. *Journal of Political Philosophy*, 12(4), 389–410.

Chambers, S. (2012) Deliberation and mass democracy. In J. Parkinson & J. Mansbridge (eds.), *Deliberative Systems: Deliberative Democracy at the Large Scale* (pp. 52–71). Cambridge: Cambridge University Press.

Chambers, S. (2017). Balancing epistemic quality and equal participation in a system approach to deliberative democracy. *Social Epistemology*, 31(3), 266–276.

Christensen, J. (2015). Recruitment and expertise in the European Commission. *West European Politics*, 38(3), 649–678.

Christensen, J. (2017). *The Power of Economists within the State*. Stanford: Stanford University Press.

Christensen, J. (2021). Expert knowledge and policymaking: A multi-disciplinary research agenda. *Policy & Politics*, 49(3), 455–471.

Christensen, J., & Gornitzka, Å. (Forthcoming 2022). Expertise in EU policy-making. In P. Graziano & J. Tosun (eds.), *Encyclopedia of European Union Public Policy*. Cheltenham: Edward Elgar.

Christensen, J., & Hesstvedt, S. (2019). Expertisation or greater representation? Evidence from Norwegian advisory commissions. *European Politics and Society*, 20(1), 83–100.

Christensen, J., Hesstvedt, S., Holst, C., Christiansen, P.M., Holli, A.M., & Pronin, K. (2022). Expert participation on Nordic advisory commissions: a comparative analysis. Working paper.

Christensen, J., & Holst, C. (2017). Advisory commissions, academic expertise and democratic legitimacy: The case of Norway. *Science and Public Policy*, 44(6), 821–833.

Christensen, J., & Holst, C. (2020). How do advocacy think tanks relate to academic knowledge? The case of Norway. *Scandinavian Political Studies*, 43(3), 223–239.

Christensen, J., & Holst, C. (2021). The Europeanization of national knowledge regimes. In V. Abazi et al. (eds.), *The Contestation of Expertise in the European Union* (pp. 47–66). London: Palgrave Macmillan.

Christensen, J., & Mandelkern, R. (2022). The technocratic tendencies of economists in government bureaucracy. *Governance*, 35(1), 233–257.

Christiano, T. (2008). *The Constitution of Equality. Democratic Authority and Its Limits*. Oxford: Oxford University Press.

Christiano, T. (2012). Rational deliberation among experts and citizens. In J. Parkinson & J. Mansbridge (eds.), *Deliberative Systems: Deliberative Democracy at the Large Scale* (pp. 27–51). Cambridge: Cambridge University Press.

Collins, H., & Evans, R. (2007). *Rethinking Expertise*. Chicago, IL: University of Chicago Press.

Craft, J., & Halligan, J. (2017). Assessing 30 years of Westminster policy advisory system experience. *Policy Sciences*, 50(1), 47–62.

Craft, J., & Howlett, M. (2013). The dual dynamics of policy advisory systems: The impact of externalization and politicization on policy advice. *Policy and Society*, 32(3), 187–197.

Crouch, C. (2004). *Post-Democracy*. Cambridge: Polity Press.

Chwieroth, J.M. (2010). *Capital Ideas: The IMF and the Rise of Financial Liberalization*. Princeton, NJ: Princeton University Press.

Dahl, R. (1985). *Controlling Nuclear Weapons: Democracy versus Guardianship*. Syracuse, NY: SUNY Press.

Dahl, R. (1989). *Democracy and Its Critics*. New Haven, CT: Yale University Press.

Dahlström, C., Lundberg, E., & Pronin, K. (2021). No more political compromise? Swedish Commissions of Inquiry 1990–2016. *Scandinavian Political Studies* 44(4), 416–440.

Davies, H., Nutley, S., & Smith, P. (2000). *What Works? Evidence-Based Policy and Practice in Public Services*. Bristol: Bristol University Press.

De Francesco, F. (2018). "The impact of private consultancies in EU governance: A document analysis of the impact assessment concerning the liberalisation of rail passenger service". Paper presented at the 2018 ECPR General Conference, Hamburg, August 22–25.

Dewey, J. (1927/1991). *The Public and Its Problems*. Chicago: Swallow Press.
Dietelhoff, N. (2009). Deliberation. In H.Brunkhorst, R. Kriede, & C. Lafont (eds.), *Habermas-Handbuch* (p. 301). Stuttgart: Verlag J.B. Metzler.
Douglas, H. (2009). *Science, Policy, and the Value-Free Ideal*. Pittsburgh, PA: University of Pittsburgh Press.
Dowding, K., & Taflaga, M. (2020). Career de-separation in Westminster democracies. *Political Quarterly*, 91(1), 116–124.
Dupré, J. (2007). Fact and value. In H. Kincaid, J. Dupré, & A. Wylie (eds.), *Value-Free Science? Ideals and Illusions* (pp. 27–41). Oxford: Oxford University Press.
Dutch Safety Board (2022). Approach to COVID-19 crisis – Part 1: through to September 2020. The Hague: Dutch Safety Board.
Dryzek, J., Bächtiger, A., Chambers, S., Cohen, J., Druckman, J. N., Felicetti, A., Fishkin, J. S., Fung, A., & Warren, M. E. (2019). The crisis of democracy and the science of deliberation. *Science*, 363, 1144–1146.
Earle, J., Moran, C., & Ward-Perkins, Z. (2017). *The Econocracy. The Perils of Leaving Economics to the Experts*. Manchester: Manchester University Press.
Eddy, D.M. (1982). Probabilistic reasoning in clinical medicine: Problems and opportunities. In D. Kahneman, P. Slovic, & A. Tversky (eds.), *Judgment Under Uncertainty: Heuristics and Biases* (pp. 249–267). Cambridge: Cambridge University Press.
Elster, J. (1995). Strategic uses of argument. In K. Arrow, R. Mnookin, L. Ross, A. Tversky, & R. Wilson (eds.), *Barriers to Conflict Resolutio* (pp. 236–257). New York: Norton.
Elster, J. (1998). Introduction. In J. Elster (ed.), *Deliberative Democracy* (pp. 1–18). Cambridge: Cambridge University Press.
Elster, J. (2000). Arguing and bargaining in two constituent assemblies. *University of Pennsylvania Journal of Constitutional Law*, 2, 345–421.
Elster, J. (2013). *Securities against Misrule*. Cambridge: Cambridge University Press.
Eriksen, A. (2020). The political literacy of experts. *Ratio Juris*, 33(1), 82–97.
Estlund, D. (1993). Making truth safe for democracy. In D. Copp, J. Hampton, & J. Roemer (eds.), *The Idea of Democracy* (pp. 71–100). Cambridge: Cambridge University Press.
Estlund, D. (1997). Beyond fairness and deliberation: The epistemic dimension of democratic authority. In J. Bohman & W. Rehg (eds.), *Deliberative Democracy: Essays on Reason and Politic* (173–204). Cambridge: MIT Press.
Estlund, D. (2008). *Democratic Authority: A Philosophical Framework*. Princeton, NJ: Princeton University Press.
Estlund, D., & Larmore, H. (2018). The epistemic value of democratic deliberation. In A. Bächtiger, J.S. Dryzek, J. Mansbridge, & M. Warren (eds.), *The Oxford Handbook of Deliberative Democracy* (pp. 113–131). Oxford: Oxford University Press.
European Central Bank (2022) Working papers. URL: www.ecb.europa.eu/pub/research/working-papers/html/index.en.html (accessed on June 15, 2022)

European Commission. (2001). *Democratizing Expertise and Establishing Scientific Reference Systems*. Report of the Working Group 1b, final version, 2 July. Brussels: European Commission.

European Commission. (2002). *Improving the Knowledge Base for Better Policies. Communication from the Commission on the Collection and Use of Expertise: Principles and Guidelines*. COM (2002) 713 final, 11 December. Brussels: European Commission.

European Commission. (2009). *Notes to Directors Generals and Heads of Services – Evaluation Report on the Horizontal Rules within the Framework for Commission's Expert Groups*. SEC (2009) 486 final, 2 April. Brussels: European Commission.

European Commission. (2010). *Communication from the President to the Commission – Framework for Commission Expert Groups: Horizontal Rules and Public Register*. C (2010) 7649 final, 10 November. Brussels: European Commission.

European Commission. (2022). Regulatory Scrutiny Board. URL: https://ec.eur opa.eu/info/law/law-making-process/regulatory-scrutiny-board_en (accessed on September 9, 2022)

Fawcett, P., Flinders, M., Hay, C., & Wood, M. (Eds.). (2017). *Anti-Politics, Depoliticization, and Governance*. Oxford: Oxford University Press.

Feldman, M.S., & March, J.G. (1981). Information in organizations as signal and symbol. *Administrative Science Quarterly*, 26(2), 171–186.

Fischer, F. (1990). *Technocracy and the Politics of Expertise*. Newbury Park, CA: Sage.

Fischer, F. (2009). *Democracy & Expertise: Reorienting Policy Analysis*. Oxford: Oxford University Press.

Fishkin, J.S. (2009). *When the People Speak: Deliberative Democracy and Public Consultation*. Oxford: Oxford University Press.

Flauss, D. (2021). *Radical Proceduralism. Democracy from Philosophicl Principles to Political Institutions*. Bingley: Emerald Publishing.

Folketinget (2021). Håndteringen af covid-19 i foråret 2020. Rapport fra en udredningsgruppe. Copenhagen: Folketinget.

Føllesdal, A., & Ulfstein, G. (2018). International Courts and Tribunals. Rise and Reaction. *The Judicialization of International Law: A Mixed Blessing?* Oxford Scholarship Online

Forst, R. (2001). The rule of reason. Three models of deliberative democracy. *Ratio Juris*, 14(4), 345–378.

Forst, R. (2021). Normativität und Wirklichkeit. Zu einer kritisch-realistisch Theorie der Politik. In *Normative Ordnungen*. Herausgegeben von Rainer Forst und Klaus Günther (pp. 74–93). Berlin: Suhrkamp.

Foucault, M. (2001). *Fearless Speech*. Los Angeles, CA: Semiotext(e).

Fourcade, M. (2006). The construction of a global profession. *American Journal of Sociology*, 112(1), 145–194.

Fricker, M., Graham, P.J., Henderson, D., & Pedersen, N.J.L.L. (2020). *The Routledge Handbook of Social Epistemology*. New York and Oxon: Routledge.

Galanti, M.T., & Lippi, A. (2022). Government research institutes in the Italian policy advisory system. *International Review of Administrative Sciences* (early view).

Geddes, M. (2021). The webs of belief around 'evidence'in legislatures: The case of select committees in the UK House of Commons. *Public Administration,* 99(1), 40–54.

Gesang, B. (2010). Are moral philosophers moral experts? *Bioethics,* 24(4), 153–159.

Gibbons, M. et al. (1994). *The New Production of Knowledge: The Dynamics of Science and Research in Contemporary Societies.* London: SAGE Publications.

Giddens, A. (1990). *The Consequences of Modernity.* Oxford: Polity Press:

Goldman, A. (2001/2011). Experts: Which ones should you trust? In A. Goldman & D. Whitcomb (eds.). *Social Epistemology. Essential Readings* (183–217) Oxford: Oxford University Press. First published in *Philosophy and Phenomenological Research,* 63(1), 85–11.

Goldman, A., & Whitcomb, D. (Eds.). (2011.) *Social Epistemology: Essential Readings.* Oxford: Oxford University Press.

Goodin, R., & List, C. (2001). Epistemic democracy: Generalizing the Condorcet Jury Theorem. *Journal of Political Philosophy,* 9(3), 277–306.

Gornitzka, Å., & Krick, E. (2018). The expertisation of stakeholder involvement in the EU. In C. Holst, M. Warat, & M. Gora (eds.), *Expertization and Democracy in Europe.* London: Routledge.

Gornitzka, Å., & Sverdrup, U. (2011). Access of experts: information and EU decision-making. *West European Politics,* 34(1), 48–70.

Gross, N. (2013). *Why Are Professors Liberal and Why Do Conservatives Care?* Cambridge, MA: Harvard University Press.

Grundmann, R. (2016). The problem of expertise in knowledge societies. *Minerva,* 55, 25–48.

Gundersen, T. (2018). Scientists as experts: A distinct role? *Studies in History and Philosophy of Science Part A,* 69, 52–59.

Gundersen, T. (2022). Values in expert reasoning: A pragmatic approach. In E.O. Eriksen (ed.), *The Accountability of Experts: Making the Unelected Safe for Democracy.* Oxford: Routledge.

Gundersen, T. & Holst, C. (2022). Trusted, but not trustworthy? Science advice in an environment of trust. *Social Epistemology* (Online First)

Gundersen, T. et al. (2022). A new dark age? Truth, trust, and environmental science. *Annual Review Environment and Resources.*

Gutmann, A., & Thompson, D. (1996). *Democracy and Disagreement.* Cambridge, MA: Harvard University Press.

Gutmann, A., & Thompson, D. (2005). *Why Deliberative Democracy?* Princeton, NJ: Princeton University Press.

Haas, P.M. (1992). Introduction: Epistemic communities and international policy coordination. *International Organization,* 46(1), 1–35.

Habermas, J. (1968/1974). The scientization of politics and public opinion. In J. Habermas, *Toward a Rational Society.* Boston, MA: Beacon Press.

Habermas, J. (1972/1984). Wahrheitstheorien. In J. Habermas (ed.), *Vorstudien und Ergänzungen zur Theorie des kommunikativen Handelns*. Frankfurt am Main: Suhrkamp.

Habermas, J. (1996). *Between Facts and Norms: Contributions to a Discourse Theory of Law and Democracy*. Cambridge, MA: MIT Press.

Habermas, J. (2001). *The Post-national Constellation*. Cambridge, MA: MIT Press.

Habermas, J. (2007). Kommunikative Rationalität und grenzüberschreitende Politik: eine Replik. In P. Niesen & B. Herborth (eds.), *Anarchie der kommunikativen Freiheit. Jürgen Habermas und die Theorie der internationalen Politik*. Frankfurt am Main: Suhrkamp.

Habermas, J. (2009). Political communication in media society – Does democracy still have an epistemic dimension? The impact of normative theory on empirical research Europe. In J. Habermas, *Europe. A Faltering Project?* Oxford: Polity Press.

Habermas, J. (2013). Stichworte zu einer Diskurstheorie des Rechts und des demokratischen Rechtstaates. In J. Habermas, *Im Sog der Technokratie*. Berlin: Suhrkamp.

Hardwig, J. (1985). Epistemic dependence. *Journal of Philosophy*, 82(7), 335–349.

Hardwig, J. (1991). The role of trust in knowledge. *Journal of Philosophy*, 88(12), 693–708.

Hayek, F.A. (1937). Economics and knowledge. *Economica*, 4(13).33–54

Hayek, F.A. (1945). The use of knowledge in society. *American Economic Review*, 35(4), 519–530.

Hayek, F.A. (1949). The intellectuals and socialism. *University of Chicago Law Review*, 16(3), 417–433.

Head, B.W. (2015). Toward more evidence-informed policy-making. *Public Administration Review*, 76(3), 472–484.

Head, B.W., Ferguson, M., Cherney, A., & Boreham, P. (2014). Are policymakers interested in social research? *Policy and Society*, 33, 89–101.

Heath, J. (2020). *The Machinery of Government*. Oxford: Oxford University Press.

Heclo, H. (1974). *Modern Social Politics in Britain and Sweden: From Relief to Income Maintenance*. New Haven, CT, and London: Yale University Press.

Herzog, L. (2020). Two challenges for participatory deliberative democracy: Expertise and the workplace. *Krisis*, 40(1), 91–98.

Hesstvedt, S., & Christensen, J. (2021). Political and administrative control of expert groups—A mixed-methods study. *Governance* (early view).

Hesstvedt, S., & Christiansen, P.M. (2022). The politics of policy inquiry commissions: Denmark and Norway, 1971–2017. *West European Politics*, 45(2), 430–454.

Hirschi, C. (2018). *Skandal-Experten, Experten-Skandalen. Zur Geschichte eines Gegenwartsproblems*. Berlin: Matthes & Seitz Berlin.

Hoffman, M. (2012). How to identify moral experts? An application of Goldman's criteria for expert identification to the domain of morality. *Analyse & Kritik: Zeitschrift für Sozialtheorie*, 34(2), 299–313.

Højlund, S. (2015). Evaluation in the European Commission: For accountability or learning? *European Journal of Risk Regulation*, 6(1), 35–46.

Holst, C. & Christensen, J. (2022). The epistemic quality of expert bodies: From normative-theoretical concept to empirical measurement. Under review.

Holst, C. & Langvatn, S. (2021). Descriptive representation of women in international courts, *Journal of Social Philosophy*, 52(4), 473–490.

Holst, C. & Molander, A. (2009). Freedom of expression and freedom of discourse. examining a justificatory strategy. In: *Freedom of Speech Abridged? Cultural, Legal and Philosophical Challenges*. Ed. A. Kierulf and H. Rønning. Gothenburg: NORDICOM.

Holst, C., & Molander, A. (2017). Public deliberation and the fact of expertise: Making experts accountable. *Social Epistemology*, 31(3), 235–250.

Holst, C., & Molander, A. (2018). Asymmetry, disagreement and biases: Epistemic worries about expertise. *Social Epistemology*, 32(6), 358–371.

Holst, C., & Molander, A. (2020). Epistemic democracy and the role of experts. *Contemporary Political* Theory, 18(4), 541–561.

Holst, C., & Molander, A. (2021). Responding to crises—worries about expertization. In: Riddervold, M., Trondal, J., Newsome, A. (eds) *The Palgrave Handbook of EU Crises. Palgrave Studies in European Union Politics*. Palgrave Macmillan.

Howlett, M., & Migone, A. (2013). Policy advice through the market: The role of external consultants in contemporary policy advisory systems. *Policy and Society*, 32(3), 241–254.

Jabko, N. (2003). Democracy in the age of the euro. *Journal of European Public Policy*, 10(5), 710–739.

Jabko, N. (2010). The hidden face of the Euro. *Journal of European Public Policy*, 17(3), 318–334.

Jasanoff, S. (1998). *The Fifth Branch. Science Advisors as Policymakers*. Cambridge, MA: Harvard University Press.

Jasanoff, S. (Ed.). (2004). *States of Knowledge*. Abingdon, UK: Taylor & Francis.

Jasanoff, S. (2005). *Designs on Nature: Science and Democracy in Europe and the United States*. Princeton, NJ: Princeton University Press.

Jasanoff, S. (2012). *Science and Public Reason*. London: Routledge.

Jasanoff, S. et al. (2021). *Comparative Covid Response: Crisis, Knowledge, Politics. Interim Report*. Ithaca, NY: Cornell University.

Jeffrey, A. (2017). Limited epistocracy and political inclusion. *Episteme*, 15(4), 412–432.

Kahneman, D. (2012). *Thinking, Fast and Slow*. London: Penguin Books.

Karpowitz, C.F., & Mendelberg, T. (2018). The political psychology of deliberation. In *Oxford Handbook of Deliberative Democracy* (pp. 535–555). Oxford: Oxford University Press.

Kelly, J.T. (2012). *Framing Democracy: A Behavioral Approach to Democratic Theory*. Princeton and Oxford: Princeton University Press.

Kelsen, H. (1925/1945). *General Theory of Law and State*. Cambridge, MA: Harvard University Press 1945, 259–260.

Kelstrup, J.D. (2018). Think tanks in EU public policies. In H. Heinelt & S. Münch (eds.), *Handbook of European Policies: Interpretive Approaches to the EU* (pp. 353–370). Cheltenham: Edward Elgar.

Keohane, R.O., Lane, M., and Oppenheimer M. (2014). The Ethics of Scientific Communication under Uncertainty. *Politics, Philosophy & Economics,* 13(4), 343–368.

Kitcher, P. (1990). The division of cognitive of labor. *Journal of Philosophy,* 87(1), 2–22.

Kitcher, P. (2011). *Science in a Democratic Society.* New York, NY: Prometheus Books.

Knutsen, O. (Ed.). (2017). *The Nordic Models in Political* Science: Challenged, but Still Viable? Bergen: Fagbokforlaget.

Koppl, R. (2018). *Expert Failures.* Cambridge: Cambridge University Press.

Krick, E. (2015). Negotiated expertise in policy-making. How governments use hybrid advisory committees. *Science and Public Policy,* 42(4), 487–500.

Krick, E. (2021). *Expertise and Participation: Institutional Designs for Policy Development in Europe.* London: Palgrave Macmillan.

Krick, E., Christensen, J. & Holst, C. (2019): "Between 'scientisation' and a 'participatory turn'. Tracing shifts in the governance of policy advice", *Science and Public Policy* 46(6): 927–939.

Krick, E., & Holst, C. (2018a). Committee governance in consensus cultures: An exploration of best practice cases in Norway and Germany. In E. Fredrik et al. (eds.), *Democratic States and Democratic Societies: Institutional Change in the Nordic Model* (pp. 151–174). Berlin/Boston: De Gruyter.

Krick, E., & Holst, C. (2018b). "The socio-political ties of expert bodies", *European Politics and Society* 20(1): 117–131.

Krick, E. & Holst, C. (2020). Governance by hybrid advisory commissions – a hallmark of social democracy?, *Comparative Social Research* (Online First).

Kriesi, H.P. (2018). The implications of the euro crisis for democracy. *Journal of European Public Policy,* 25(1), 58–82.

Lafont, C. (2006). The epistemic conception of deliberative democracy defended – Reasons, rightness and equal political autonomy. In S. Besson & J.L. Marti (eds.), *The Discontents of Deliberative Democracy.* London: Routledge.

Lafont, C. (2019). *Democracy without Shortcuts: A Participatory Conception of Deliberative Democracy.* Oxford: Oxford University Press.

Lafont, C. (2020). Sticking to the long road of participatory democracy: Replies to my critics. *Krisis,* 40(1), 144–164.

Landemore, H. (2012). *Democratic Reason: Politics, Collective Intelligence, and the Rule of the Many.* Princeton, NJ: Princeton University Press.

Landemore, H. (2020). *Open Democracy: Reinventing Popular Rule for the Twenty-First Century.* Princeton, Princeton University Press.

Lane, M. (2014). When the experts are uncertain: Scientific knowledge and the ethics of democratic judgment. *Episteme,* 11(1), 97–118.

Lamont, M. (2009). *How Professors Think: Inside the Curious World of Academic Judgment.* Cambridge, MA: Harvard University Press.

Larmore, C. (2020). *What Is Political Philosophy?* Princeton, NJ: Princeton University Press.

Legard, S., & Goldfrank, B. (2021). The systemic turn and participatory budgeting: The case of Rio Grande do sul. *Journal of Latin American Studies*, 35, 161–187.

Lincoln, A. (2009). Adress at Gettisburg, Pennsylvania, Nov. 19, 1863. In A. Delblanco (ed.), *The Portable Abraham Lincoln*. London: Penguin. 323.

Lippert-Rasmussen, K. (2012). Estlund on epistocracy: A critique. *Res Publica*, 18(3), 441–458.

Lippman, W. (1925). *The Phantom Public*. New York: MacMillan.

Littoz-Monnet, A. (2020). *Governing through Expertise*. Cambridge: Cambridge University Press.

Locke, J. (1690/1997). *An Essay Concerning Human Understanding*. Ed. By R. Woolhouse. London: Penguin Books.

Longino, H.E. (2002). *The Fate of Knowledge*. Princeton: Princeton University Press.

Madeline, B., & Charrel, M. (2020). Jean Tirole : "Le grand danger serait d'oublier l'avenir de la France et de l'Europe" dans la réponse à la crise. *Le Monde*, May 28.

Madison, J. (1787/1987). Federalist papers, Number 10 and 63. In J. Madison, A. Hamilton and J. Jay, *Federalist Papers*, edited by Isaac Kramnick. London: Penguin Books.

Mair, P. (2013). *Ruling the Void: The Hollowing of Western Democracy*. London: Verso.

Majone, G. (1996). *Regulating Europe*. London: Routledge.

Mansbridge, J., Bohman, J., Chambers, S., Christiano, T., Fung, A., Parkinson, J., Thompson, D.F., & Warren, M.E. (2012). A systemic approach to deliberative democracy. In J. Parkinson & J. Mansbridge (eds.), *Deliberative Systems: Deliberative Democracy at the Large Scale* (pp. 1–26). Cambridge: Cambridge University Press.

Mansbridge, J, & Macedo, S. (2019) Populism and Democratic Theory. *Annual Review of Law and Social Science*, 15, 59–77.

Mannheim, K. (1936). *Ideology and Utopia*. London: Routledge & Kegan Paul.

Marcussen, M. (2006). Scientization of central banking as a case study. In T. Christensen & P. Lægreid (eds.), *Autonomy and Regulation: Coping with Agencies in the Modern State)*. Cheltenham: Edward Elgar.

Markoff, J., & Montecinos, V. (1993). The ubiquitous rise of economists. *Journal of Public Policy*, 13(1), 37–68.

Marti, J.L. (2006). The epistemic conception of deliberative democracy defended reasons, rightness and equal political autonomy. In S. Besson & J.L. Marti (eds.), *The Discontents of Deliberative Democracy*. London: Routledge.

Marti, J.L. (2013). "Why (deliberative) democracy has epistemic value and why that is not enough to justify it". Paper presented at the EPISTO Conference, Oslo, April 2013.

McGann, J.G. (2020). 2019 Global Go To Think Tank Index Report.

McPhilemy, S., & Moschella, M. (2019). Central banks under stress: Reputation, accountability and regulatory coherence. *Public Administration*, 97(3), 489–498.

Meade, E.E., & Stasavage, D. (2008). Publicity of debate and the incentive to dissent: Evidence from the US Federal Reserve. *Economic Journal*, 118, 695–717.

Meehl, P.E. (1954). *Clinical versus Statistical Prediction: A Theoretical Analysis and a Review of the Evidence.* Minneapolis, MN: University of Minnesota Press.

Mendelberg, T. (2002). The deliberative citizen. Theory and evidence. Ali Mendelberg. 2002. In M. Delli Carpini, L. Huddy, & R.Y. Shapiro (eds.), *Research in Micropolitics*, Volume 6: Political Decision Making, Deliberation and Participation. New York: Elsevier Press. 151–193.

Mercier, H. (2011). When experts argue: Explaining the best and the worst of reasoning. *Argumentation*, 25, 313–327.

Merton, R.K. (1942/1973). *The Sociology of Science: Theoretical and Empirical Investigations.* Chicago, IL: University of Chicago Press.

Metz, J. (2015). *The European Commission, Expert Groups, and the Policy Process: Demystifying Technocratic Governance.* New York: Springer.

Meyer, M. (2010). The rise of the knowledge broker. *Science Communication*, 32(1), 118–127.

Meynaud, J. (1968). *Technocracy.* London: Faber and Faber.

Mikalsen, K. K. (2022). Expertise and the general will in democratic republicanism. In E.O. Eriksen (ed.), *The accountability of experts. Making the unelected safe for democracy.* London: Routledge. 155–172.

Mill, J.S. (1859/1989). On liberty. In S. Collini (ed.), J.S. Mill, *'On Liberty' and Other Writings.* Cambridge: Cambridge University Press.

Mill, J.S. (1861/1991). *Considerations on Representative Government.* Amherst, New York: Prometheus.

Molander, A. (2016). *Discretion in the Welfare State: Social Rights and Professional Judgment.* London: Routledge.

Moore, A. (2014). Democratic reason, democratic faith, and the problem of expertise. *Critical Review*, 26(1–2), 101–114.

Moore, A. (2017). *Critical Elitism: Deliberation, Democracy, and the Problem of Expertise.* Cambridge: Cambridge University Press.

Moore, A. (2021). Three models of democratic expertise. *Perspectives on Politics,* 19(2), 553–563.

Moore, A., & MacKenzie, M. (2020). Policymaking during crises: How diversity and disagreement can help manage the politics of expert advice. *BMJ*, 371, m4039.

Moos, P. (2014). *An uncertain business: Industry responses to the regulation of nanotechnologies.* Doctoral dissertation. Florence: European University Institute.

Mounk, Y. (2018). *The People vs. Democracy.* Cambridge, MA: Harvard University Press.

Mudde, C. (2004). The populist Zeitgeist. *Government and Opposition,* 39(4), 541–563.

Mügge, D. (2011). From pragmatism to dogmatism: European Union governance, policy paradigms and financial meltdown. *New Political Economy*, 16(2), 185–206.

Müller, J.W. (2016). *What Is Populism?* Philadelphia, PA: Pennsylvania University Press.

Münkler, L. (2020). *Expertokratie. Zwischen Herrschaft kraft Wissens und politischem Dezisionismus.* Tübingen: Mohr Siebeck.

Mutz, D. (2008a). Is deliberative democracy a falsifiable theory? *Annual Review of Political Science,* 11, 521–538.

Mutz, D. (2008b). *Hearing the Other Side: Deliberative versus Participatory.* Cambridge: Cambridge University Press.

Myrdal, G. (1930/1953). *The Political Element in the Development of Economic Theory.* London: Routledge.

Newman, J., Cherney, A., & Head, B.W. (2016). Do policy makers use academic research? Reexamining the "two communities" theory of research utilization. *Public Administration Review,* 76(1), 24–32.

Nichols, T. (2017). *The Death of Expertise: The Campaign Against Established Knowledge and Why It Matters.* Oxford: Oxford University Press.

Nino, C.S. (1996). *The Constitution of Deliberative Democracy.* New Haven: Yale University Press.

NOU. (2012). Rapport fra 22. juli-kommisjonen. NOU 2012:14.

NOU. (2014a). Skyldevne, sakkyndighet og samfunnsvern. NOU 2014:10.

NOU. (2014b). Åpent og rettferdig – prioriteringer i helsetjenesten. NOU 2014:12.

NOU. (2014c). Kapitalbeskatning i en internasjonal økonomi. NOU 2014:13.

NOU. (2018). Kapital i omstillingens tid. NOU 2018:5.

NOU (2021). Myndighetenes håndtering av koronapendemien – rapport fra Koronakommisjonen. NOU 2021:6.

Nuzzo, R. (2014). Scientific method: Statistical errors. *Nature,* 506, 150–152.Oliver, K., et al. (2014). A systematic review of barriers to and facilitators of the use of evidence by policymakers. *BMC Health Services Research,* 14(2), 1–12.

Olsen, J.P. (2010). *Governing through Institution Building: Institutional Theory and Recent European Experiments in Democratic Organization.* Oxford: Oxford University Press.

Oreskes, N. (2019). *Why Trust Science?* Princeton, NJ: Princeton University Press.

Page, E.C., & Jenkins, B. (2005). *Policy Bureaucracy: Government with a Cast of Thousands.* Oxford: OUP.

Page, S.E. (2007). *The Difference. How the Power of Diversity Creates Better Groups, Firms, Schools, and Societies.* Princeton, NJ: Princeton University Press.

Page, E.C., & Wright, V. (Eds.). (1999). *Bureaucratic Elites in Western European States: A Comparative Analysis of Top Officials.* Oxford: Oxford University Press.

Parkhurst, J. (2017). *The Politics of Evidence: From Evidence-Based Policy to the Good Governance of Evidence.* Abingdon: Routledge.

Parkinson, J. (2018). Deliberative systems. In Bächtiger, A. et al. (eds.), *The Oxford Handbook of Deliberative Democracy.* Oxford: Oxford University Press.

122 References

Pedersen, J. (2009). Habermas and the political sciences: The relationship between theory and practice. *Philosophy of the Social Sciences*, 39(3), 381–407.

Pedersen, W., Holst, C., & Fjell, L.K. (2021). Warriors in the "war on drugs": Lay experts in Norwegian drug policy. *Current Sociology* (Online first).

Peter, F. (2008). Pure epistemic proceduralism. *Episteme*, 5(1), 33–55.

Peter, F. (2009). *Democratic Legitimacy*. New York, NY: Routledge.

Peters, B.G. (2018). *The Politics of Bureaucracy: An Introduction to Comparative Public Administration*. London and New York: Routledge.

Petersson, O. (2015). Rational politics: Commissions of inquiry and the referral system in Sweden. In J. Pierre (ed.), *The Oxford Handbook of Swedish Politics* (pp. 650–662). Oxford: Oxford University Press.

Pettit, P. (2004). Depoliticizing democracy. *Ratio Juris*, 17(1), 52–65.

Pielke, R.A. (2007). *The Honest Broker: Making Sense of Science in Policy and Politics*. Cambridge: Cambridge University Press.

Pincione, G., & Tesón, F. (2006). *Rational Choice and Democratic Deliberation: A Theory of Discourse Failure*. Cambridge: Cambridge University Press.Plato. *Statesman* (Cambridge Texts in the History of Political Thought). Ed. by J. Annas and R. Waterfield. Cambridge: Cambridge University Press, 1995.

Plato. *The Republic* (Cambridge Texts in the History of Political Thought). Ed. by G.R.F. Ferrary. Cambridge: Cambridge University Press, 2000.

Posner, R.A. (2002). *Public Intellectuals: A Study of Decline*. Cambridge: Mass.: Harvard University Press.

Prendergast, C. (1986). Alfred Schütz and the Austrian School of Economics. *American Journal of Sociology*, 92(1), 1–26.

Putnam, H. (2002). *The Collapse of the Fact/Value Dichotomy and Other Essays*. Cambridge, MA: Harvard University Press.

Quirk, P.J. (2010). The trouble with experts. *Critical Review*, 22(4), 449–465.

Rahman Khan, S. (2012). The sociology of elites. *Annual Review of Sociology*, 38, 361–377.

Rawls, J. (1993). *Political Liberalism*. New York: Columbia University Press.

Reiss, J. (2008). *Error in Economics: Towards a More Evidence-Based Methodology*. London & New York: Routledge.

Renå, H. (2017). 22. juli-kommisjonens analyse, vurderinger og konklusjoner – en metaanalyse av politiaksjon Utøya. *Norsk statsvitenskapelig tidsskrift*, 33(1), 10–36.

Renå, H., & Christensen, J. (2020). Learning from crisis: The role of enquiry commissions. *Journal of Contingencies and Crisis Management*, 28(1), 41–49.

Renn, O. (2022) Strategic Crisis Management in the EU. SAPEA Evidence Review Report (ERR).

Rich, A. (2004). *Think Tanks, Public Policy, and the Politics of Expertise*. Cambridge: Cambridge University Press.

Rickert, G. (1983). *Technokratie und Demokratie: Zum Technokratieproblem in der Staatstheorie einschliesslich der Europarechts*. Frankfurt am Main: Peter Lang.

Rinderle, P. (2014). Demokratischer Legitimität und wissenschafliche Expertise in Zeiten des Klimawandels. *Jahrbuch für Wissenschaft und Ethik*, 18, 215–231.

Rinderle, P. (2015). *Demokratie*. De Gruyter: Berlin/Boston.

Rosén, G., & Tørnblad, S.H. (2018). How does expert knowledge travel between EU institutions? The case of the Transatlantic Trade and Investment Partnership, *European Politics and Society*, 20(1), 32–48.

Rothstein, B. (1998). *Just Institutions Matter. The Moral and Political Logic of the Universal Welfare State*. Cambridge: Cambridge University Press.

Rothstein, B. (2011). *The Quality of Government*. Chicago: Chicago University Press.

Rousseau, J.J. (1762/1973). *The Social Contract and Discourses*. Translation and Introduction by G.D.H. Cole. Revised and augmented by J.H. Burmfitt and John C. Hall. London: Dent.

Rudner, R. (1953). The scientist qua scientist makes value judgments. *Philosophy of Science*, 20(1), 1–6.

Salines, M., Glöckler, G., & Truchlewski, Z. (2012). Existential crisis incremental response: The Eurozone's dual institutional evolution. *Journal of European Public Policy*, 19(5), 665–681.

Scharpf, F. (1999). *Regieren in Europa: Effektiv und demokratisch?* Frankfurt am Main.: Campus Verlag.

Schelsky, H. (1961). *Der Mensch in der wissenschaftlichen Zivilisation*. Wiesbaden: VS Verlag für Sozialwissenschaften.

Schlefer, J. (2012). *The Assumptions Economists Make*. Cambridge, MA: Harvard University Press.

Schrefler, L. (2010). The usage of scientific knowledge by independent regulatory agencies. *Governance*, 23(2), 309–330.

Schumpeter, J.A. (1942/1995). *Capitalism, Socialism & Democracy*. London: Routledge.

Schütz, A. (1946/1964). The well-informed citizen. In *Collected Papers II*. Ed. by A. Brodersen. Haag: Martin Nijhof 1965. First published in *Social Research*, 13 (1946).

Schütz, A. (1953/1962). Common-sense and scientific interpretation of human action. In *Collected Papers I*. Ed. by M. Natanson. Haag: Martinus Nijhoff 1962. First published in *Philosophy and Phenomenological Research*, Vol. 14 (1953).

Schwartzberg, M. (2015). Epistemic democracy and its challenges. *Annual Review of Political Science*, 18, 187–203.

Seibicke, H. (2020). Gender expertise in public policymaking: The European women's lobby and the EU maternity leave directive. *Social Politics*, 27(2), 385–408.

Simonsohn, U., Nelson, L.D., & Simmons, J.P. (2014). P-curve: A key to the file-drawer. *Journal of Experimental Psychology: General*, 143(2), 534.

Singer, P. (1972). Moral experts. *Analysis*, 32(4), 115–117.

Somin, I. (2013 *Democracy and Political Ignorance*. Stanford: Stanford University Press.

Streeck, W. (2014). *Buying Time: The Belated Crisis of Democratic Capitalism.* New York: Verso.

Steffek, J. (2021). *International Organization as Technocratic Utopia.* Oxford: Oxford University Press.

Stehr, N., & Grundmann, R. (2010). *Expertenwissen. Die Kultur und die Macht von Experten, Beratern und Ratgebern.* Weilerswist: Velbrück Wissenschaft.

Steiner, J. et al. (2017). *Deliberation Across Deeply Divided Societies. Transformative Moments.* Cambridge: Cambridge University Press.

Stiglitz, J.E., Edlin, A.S., & DeLong, J.B. (Eds.). (2008). *The Economists' Voice: Top Economists' Take on Today's Problems.* New York: Colombia University Press.

Sunstein, C.R. (2002). The law of group polarization. *Journal of Political Philosophy,* 10(2), 175–195.

Sunstein, C.R. (2006). *Infotopia: How Many Minds Produce Knowledge.* Oxford: Oxford University Press.

Sunstein, C.R. (2016) *The Most Knowledgeable Branch,* 164 *University of Pennsylvania Law Review,* 1607

Sunstein, C.R., & Hastie, R. (2015). *Wiser: Getting beyond Groupthink to Make Groups Smarter.* Boston, MA: Harvard Business Review Press.

Swift, A., & White, S. (2008). Political theory, social science, and real politics. In D. Leopold & M. Stears (eds.), *Political Theory. Methods and Approaches.* (pp. 49–69). Oxford: Oxford University Press.

Taleb, N.N. (2018). *Skin in the Game: Hidden Asymmetries in Daily Life.* New York: Random House.

Tellmann, S.M. (2012). The constrained influence of discourses: The case of Norwegian climate policy. *Environmental Politics,* 21(5), 734–752.

Tellmann, S.M. (2016). *Experts in public policymaking: Influential, yet constrained.* Doctoral thesis, Oslo and Akershus University College of Applied Sciences.

Tellmann, S.M. (2017). Bounded deliberation in public committees: The case of experts. *Critical Policy Studies,* 11(3), 311–329.

Tetlock, P. (2005). *Expert Political Judgment: How Good Is It? How Can We Know?* Princeton, NJ: Princeton University Press.

Tetlock, P., & Gardner, D. (2015). *Superforecasting: The Art and Science of Prediction.* New York: Crown.

Thompson, A. (2014). Does diversity trump ability? An example of the misuse of mathematics in social science. *Notices of the American Mathematical Society,* 61, 1024–1030.

Thompson, D. (2008). Deliberative democratic theory and empirical political science. *Annual Review of Political Science,* 11, 497–520.

Tranøy, K.E. (1976). Norms of inquiry: Methodologies as normative systems. In G. Ryle (ed.), *Contemporary Aspects of Philosoph* (pp. 1–13). London: Oriel Press.

Turner, S. (2003). *Liberal Democracy 3.0.* London: Sage.

Tversky, A., & Kahneman, D. (1974). Judgment under uncertainty: Heuristics and biases. *Science,* 185, 1124–1131.

Urbinati, N. (2014). *Democracy Disfigured: Opinion, Truth, and the People.* Cambridge, MA: Harvard University Press.

Van Den Berg, C., Howlett, M., Migone, A., Pemer, F., & Gunter, H.M. (2020). *Policy Consultancy in Comparative Perspective: Patterns, Nuances and Implications of the Contractor State.* Cambridge: Cambridge University Press.

Vibert, F. (2007). *The Rise of the Unelected. Democracy and the New Separation of Powers.* Cambridge: Cambridge University Press.

Viehoff, D. (2016). Authority and expertise. *Journal of Political Philosophy*, 24(4), 406–426.

Waldron, J. (1995). The Wisdom of the Multitude. Some Reflections on Book II, Chapter 11 of Aristotles' Politics. *Political Theory*, 23(4), 563–584.

Waldron, J. (1999). *Law and Disagreement.* Oxford: Oxford University Press.

Walton, D. (1997). *Appeal to Expert Opinion: Arguments from Authority.* University Park, PA: Pennsylvania State University Press.

Warren, M.E. (1996). Deliberative democracy and authority. *American Political Science Review*, 90(1), 46–60.

Weaver, R.K. (1989). The changing world of think tanks. *PS: Political Science & Politics*, 22(3), 563–578.

Weber, M. (1904/1949). Objectivity in Social Science and Social Policy . In E.A. Shils & H.A. Finch (eds.), *Social Science and Social Policy. Max Weber on the Methodology of the Social Sciences.* Illinois: Free Press.

Weber, M. (1922/1978). *Economy and Society.* Ed. by G. Roth and C. Wittich. Berkely: University of California Press.

Weingart, P. (1999). Scientific expertise and political accountability. *Science and Public Policy*, 26(3), 151–161.

Weingart, P. (2005). *Die Wissenschaft der Öffentlichkeit.* Weilerswist: Velbrück Wissenschaft.

Weiss, C.H. (1979). The many meanings of research utilization. *Public Administration Review*, 39(5), 426–431.

White, J., & L. Ypi (2016). *The Meaning of Partisanship.* Oxford: Oxford University Press.

Wildavsky, A. (1979). *Speaking Truth to Power: The Art and Craft of Policy Analysis.* London: Transaction.

Wilke, H. (2016). *Dezentrierte Demokratie. Prolegomena zur Revision politischer Steuerung.* Berlin: Suhrkamp Verlag.

Wolff, J. (2011). *Ethics and Public Policy.* London: Routledge.

Wright, J. (2019). *Pluralism and Social Epistemology in Economics.* Doctoral thesis, University of Cambridge

Wynne, B. (1992). Misunderstood misunderstanding; social identities and public uptake of science, *Public Understanding of Science*, 3(1), 281–304.

Wynne, B. (1996). May the sheep safely graze? A reflexive view of the expert–lay knowledge divide. In S. Lash, B. Szerszynski, & B. Wynne (eds.), *Risk, Environment and Modernity* (pp. 44–83). London: Sage.

Zenker, F. (2011). Experts and bias: When is the interest-based objection to expert argumentation sound? *Argumentation*, 25, 355–370.

Index